Ben Jonson (1572–1637) was born in or near London, the posthumous son of a clergyman, and was educated at Westminster School. Around 1597 he began to work for Henslowe's companies as player and playwright, and was imprisoned for his part in *The Isle of Dogs*, a satire now lost. In 1598 he killed a fellow actor in a duel, but escaped hanging by pleading benefit of clergy. His first major success was *Every Man in His Humour* (1598), with Shakespeare in the cast, and this was followed by *Every Man out of His Humour* in 1599. In 1605 he was imprisoned, and in danger of having his nose and ears slit, for his share in *Eastward Ho!* and gave evidence to the Privy Council concerning the Gunpowder Plot. Then followed the period of his major plays: *Volpone* (1605–6), *Epicoene, or The Silent Woman* (1609), *The Alchemist* (1610) and *Bartholomew Fair* (1614). From 1605 he had also been producing masques for the court, often with Inigo Jones, and, though not formally appointed the first poet laureate, the essentials of the position were conferred on him in 1616 when a pension was granted to him by James I. His collaboration with Jones ended with a quarrel in 1631, which Jonson treated in several poems. His non-dramatic verse includes *Epigrams*, *The Forest*, *Underwoods* and a translation of Horace's *Ars Poetica*.

During the reign of James I Jonson's literary prestige and influence were unrivalled. He presided over a literary circle which met at the Mermaid Tavern and his friends included Shakespeare, Chapman, Beaumont, Fletcher, Cotton and Selden. On his death he was buried in Westminster Abbey.

BEN JONSON

Selected Poetry

Edited with an Introduction
and Notes by
GEORGE PARFITT

PENGUIN BOOKS

PENGUIN BOOKS

Published by the Penguin Group
Penguin Books Ltd, 27 Wrights Lane, London w8 5tz, England
Penguin Books USA Inc., 375 Hudson Street, New York, New York 10014, USA
Penguin Books Australia Ltd, Ringwood, Victoria, Australia
Penguin Books Canada Ltd, 10 Alcorn Avenue, Toronto, Ontario, Canada m4v 3b2
Penguin Books (NZ) Ltd, 182–190 Wairau Road, Auckland 10, New Zealand

Penguin Books Ltd, Registered Offices: Harmondsworth, Middlesex, England

This selection first published in Penguin Books 1992
1 3 5 7 9 10 8 6 4 2

Selection, Introduction and Notes copyright © George Parfitt, 1992
All rights reserved

Filmset in 10 on 11 pt Monophoto Ehrhardt by
Clays Ltd, St Ives plc

Printed in England by Clays Ltd, St Ives plc

Contents

CONTENTS

THE FOREST

UNDERWOODS

CONTENTS

INTRODUCTION

Ben Jonson was born in 1572 and died in 1637. His background
and early life are obscure, but much of his adult life was highly
visible and he was buried in Westminster Abbey, this being
a formalization in death of his distinction in life. His writing career began in the 1590s and continued till his death.
When he was born over twenty years of the reign of Elizabeth
I were left; when he died the Civil War was less than five years
away.

Jonson was one of the most successful writers of the Elizabethan and Jacobean periods, if the measure of success is taken
to be the length of the line from obscurity to the centre of the
court. Jonson began life with his natural father dead and had a
Westminster bricklayer as step-father, yet he became, for a
good stretch of his life, the most prominent writer of Court
masques and a royal pensioner, as well as a major cultural
authority. Between birth and death, however, he was many
other things as well: a bricklayer, a soldier, an actor, a playwright, a homicide, a changer of religion, a scholar – and a
poet. His life can be summarized as a struggle – between his
vision of what a writer should be (wise, serene, judicious) and
the realities of his personality (violent, impatient, opinionated);
and between his view of what a society should be (hierarchical,
harmonious, responsible and stable) and his sense of what
his contemporary society was (vital, turbulent, fractious and
factious).

Jonson had his triumphs and admirers, but also his disasters
and detractors. His career as a writer of masques was successful
for a considerable period, but eventuated in the famous quarrel
with Inigo Jones, who came off the better, at least in terms of
favour at Court. As a dramatist Jonson never achieved reliable
popular success. His marriage to Anne Lewis in 1594, made
when he was young by the standards of Elizabethan marital

practice, seems to have been unstable. Jonson was in prison in 1597, for his involvement with the lost play *The Isle of Dogs*; in 1598 for killing the actor Gabriel Spencer in a duel; and in 1605–6 for alleged anti-Scots aspersions in *Eastward Ho!*: this is not the full catalogue of Jonson's difficulties with the law. More domestically, his library was destroyed by fire in 1623 and he was paralysed by a stroke in 1628.

This was the violent and aggressive life of a man who survived as a professional writer. As a young adult, Jonson seems to have laid bricks, served as a soldier in the Netherlands, and acted, but once he got a start as a writer he appears to have had no other full-time occupation. His poems belong within the context of his other literary work and this total output is best seen in materialist terms.

It is accurate, I think, to regard Jonson as resentful of such defining terms. His disputes with the public about how his plays were received and his conflict with Jones about control of masque-making, together with the evidence of periods of abstinence from the stage (as between 1616 and 1626), suggest irritation at his dependence upon material circumstances. This dependence is obvious enough in relation to plays and masques. Stage drama in England was strongly audience led: employment as a writer for the stage necessitated attention to public taste, and payment for writing plays was too low for early retirement on the profits. Court masques paid considerably better, but commissions depended upon pleasing the commissioning agent and the courtly audience.

For someone like Jonson, however, poems were also necessarily related (as publications) to being a dependant. Poems are a part of what is involved in being a professional writer. Most specifically, they exist within the network of patronage. When Jonson addresses poems to Robert Sidney or Robert Wroth he is hardly in a position to ignore the brute fact that such men have power which he lacks, while the desire to give advice to a new king ('A Panegyre') has to take into account the desirability of attracting that king's favourable opinion. Both the tact and the quality of work contribute to one's chances of gaining and retaining patronage Jonson became a valuable property, and he showed considerable integrity within the context of patronage, but he could never forget his lack of independence. There is clear evidence that he worked hard to have his texts seen as objects of dignity and worth (hence the 1616 Folio and the elaborate printed texts of masques). In so doing, Jonson achieved a lot for the status of the professional writer: the effort not only enhanced Jonson's value in the market but indicated how much he needed the market to enable him to live and write.

If the poems are to be seen as part of the whole output conceived in material terms, they are also parts of the whole in other ways as well. Jonson seems to have written poems throughout his writing life: they thread their way through the oeuvre. More important, they need to be seen both as epitomizing Jonson's literary effort and as asking to be read in conjunction with his other work. They have no special status (over plays, masques or prose) in relation to Jonson's private life and opinions: they are not confessional verse. If the representation of genteel irresponsibility in *The Alchemist* were seen as shaped by the wish to please London citizens in 1610, it would be necessary to balance that view by saying that the representation of genteel responsibility in 'To Penshurst' was shaped by the wish to please the Sidney family. It would be naïve to see either play or poem as a definitive statement of Jonson's beliefs: both are too much conditioned by material factors for that to be possible. Jonson's poems are as public as his plays and masques: they all dramatize and they all have their audiences.

These poems are also very various. As a professional, Jonson is an experimenter who manifests a wish to master a variety of modes. Like his contemporary, John Donne, he has little interest in the love-sonnet or the epic, but his output includes the naturalization of the epigram and the ode, verse epistle, elegy, epithalamion, songs and a variety of lyric forms. Moreover, Jonson achieved excellence in almost every mode he attempted. The price he paid was high in the nineteenth century when, to critics and scholars alike, so much diversity of skill seemed like a lack of 'divine afflatus'.

3

Lyric Jonson is fully represented in this selection, and readers will notice how many of the lyrics are songs from plays and masques. The masque, in particular, was a highly formalized genre, dealing in abstractions and qualities rather than in personalities; and it was also highly polished, aiming to demonstrate harmonious beauty. Jonson's lyrics are superb miniatures of art – *made* objects of great classical beauty (although he was also capable of creating fine comic and popular lyrics, using, for example, Skeltonics and ballad form). These poems are not private, let alone intimate, work.

But although Jonson was a very talented writer of lyrics, with a delicacy of touch that is intriguing given the roughcast face and body, the record suggests that his main interests lay elsewhere, in modes that have a more obvious bearing on the daily life of late sixteenth- and early seventeenth-century London.

If the lyric is a short, songlike poem, the epigram exists in an interesting relationship to it. Like the lyric it is expected to be short and, insofar as lyric is associated with ideas of praise, the epigram is at times also laudatory. But epigram is more commonly linked with satire, and so with subversion of the world of ideals and worthy achievement. It is not a form which receives much attention today (although there are contemporary poets who translate epigrams) and it is perhaps rather a shock to hear Jonson describe his epigrams as the 'ripest of my studies', but the remark remains suggestive. Jonson may partly be indicating the seriousness of his attempt to follow Martial and the *Greek Anthology* in English, and partly responding to the challenge of brevity for, although Jonson is often seen as a prolix writer, he is also interested in the concentrated, terse ('epigrammatic') statement. It can also be claimed that there are outstanding poems among Jonson's epigrams. Certainly, 'On My First Son' is one of the finest poems of loss in English and 'On Spies' one of the most devastating triplets. But such a claim, stressing the quality of individual poems, may be misleading, for *Epigrams* is best seen as a single work, a collection of pieces along the lines of, for example, Sidney's *Astrophel and Stella* or Tennyson's *In Memoriam* (though very different in effect from either). From this point of view any selection from *Epigrams* is a misrepresentation. With this in mind I have chosen to include the first thirty poems *en bloc* to suggest how the collection works, and have then made a selection from the rest of Jonson's epigrams.

Taken as a whole, or even as a selection, Jonson's epigrams display very well both major drives of his poetry, towards idealization and towards what satire sees – the world as corrupt and degenerate. But because the poems fall so readily into these two categories, the real plot of *Epigrams* is to be found between these poems, in the spaces. A reader, relating both poems of praise and satirical epigrams to humankind, is called upon to mediate, while the epitaphs scattered through the collection remind the reader of how time erodes both worthlessness and value.

The valuable, the worthless and time constitute Jonson's major themes, binding and troubling the poems of *The Forest* and *Underwoods*. These poems are almost always less pure than the epigrams, in that the constituents usually co-exist within the individual poem, although this co-existence takes various forms. Types of grossness disturb the lyric worlds of 'My Picture Left in Scotland' and 'To Charis'. In 'To Penshurst' the idealization which praises the Sidneys may seek to drive satire to the margins, but it remains vitally present, in ostentatious buildings, non-residence and the lack of true hospitality and moral worth. It is striking how often Jonson approaches praise by way of satire; for example, in the opening of 'Epistle to Elizabeth . . .', or of 'To Sir Robert Wroth'. The effort to clear the ground for praise suggests how precarious and precious true worth is, and how crowded by worthlessness. And there are poems where satire dominates and where Jonson's talent for busy, compressed physical detail leads to writing of the quality of *The Alchemist* or *Volpone*. Yet Jonson avoids formal verse satire, the avoidance signalling, I think, resistance to the full cynicism of the malcontent. 'An Epistle to a Friend, to Persuade Him to the Wars' has a satiric force that suggests imminent swamping of all virtue and the threat is enacted by how much of the poem is dominated by the satiric details, as well as by the desperate nature of the suggested remedy: participation in war. Yet the poem's last paragraph reasserts Jonson's faith in the morality of self-knowledge, consistency and public responsibility. The positives survive under great pressure, but they do survive. Perhaps Jonson is closest to despair in 'A Speech according to Horace', a poem which includes possibly his most disillusioned account of the gentry and which ends with an extraordinary, haunting image:

> . . . whilst tottered virtue holds
> Her broken arms up, to their empty moulds.

But virtue is 'tottered' rather than fallen, and the poem has invoked a sense of what the gentry could and should be.

Jonson is not a difficult poet in the way in which John Donne is difficult. His syntax is usually less convoluted, his chosen verse forms are less intricate, and he seldom uses Donne's volleying of images or rapid shifts of tone and perspective. Yet his verse has its own kind of difficulty. Many poems are addressed to historical persons who are no longer familiar; Jonson uses a lot of allusion, some of it arcane; he frequently draws in detail upon classical sources, and the classics are decayed in our time; and he often writes very long verse-sentences with a battery of subordinate clauses. Even the lucidity and directness of so much of his verse (especially when taken with his socio-ethical interests) can be a source of difficulty, his concern with surfaces leading readers to confuse it with superficiality. Donne is often obviously difficult, but the striking attack and flourish of his writing fascinate many readers, even while they are baffled. Jonson may just seem plain – difficult in the ways sketched above, without the fireworks that compensate in Donne. It takes some patience to appreciate how rigorously Jonson works to mediate his impulses to optimism and despair, and how precisely the effort is recorded. The rewards, however, are great: learning to read Jonson is learning to read poetry.

It is widely understood that Jonson was a classicist; and, indeed, it is not difficult to show that he persistently draws upon classical sources. The nature of his classicism, however, has often been misunderstood. It is important, first of all, to remember that Elizabethan and Jacobean education was strongly classical in orientation: Jonson's classicism is unusual in degree, not in kind. Part of what is unusual about it is the degree to which it is assimilated, becoming an important part of Jonson's equipment as a commentator on his times. For Jonson does not usually draw attention to his borrowings from the classics: frequently a loan is only discernible by a reader with classical learning. A good example is one of Jonson's most famous lyrics, 'Drink to me, only, with thine eyes', which has a seamless lucidity and seems entirely English, but which is made up of a tissue of borrowings from the Greek prose of Philostratus. Another example is the superb epitaph 'On My First Son'. The poem's occasion – the death of the poet's son – could scarcely be more personal, and it builds to a careful, rather bitter, distinction between loving and liking:

> all his vows be such,
> As what he loves may never like too much.

The last line is a loan from the Roman poet Martial. Similarly, the last line of 'To Penshurst' is an elaboration of another moment in Martial. Or there is the fine 'An Epistle to Sir Edward Sackville', the first 80 or so lines of which Jonson has largely fashioned from Seneca's *De Beneficiis*. Close inspection of what Jonson takes from Seneca here indicates considerable selectivity and a confident command of the Latin material.

Although Jonson does use classical allusions, some of which are clearly signalled as such, his more important practice is to assimilate what is borrowed to the English texture of his verse. It should be added that much of what Jonson borrows is in the area of ethics. He uses Latin (or, more rarely Greek) ethical statements to give weight to his analysis of the contemporary English situation. The weight, as in the example from 'To Penshurst', may be felt by a reader with little or no classical knowledge, but the full authority will only be recognized by those who possess such knowledge; and this knowledge is an intimate part of Jonson's constitution. One of his rare religious poems, 'To Heaven', exemplifies this further. Near its end Jonson signals a borrowing from the apostle Paul:

> Yet dare I not complain, or wish for death
> With holy Paul . . .

What he has not signalled is that a couplet just before this –

> I feel my griefs too, and there scarce is ground,
> Upon my flesh to inflict another wound.

– is adapted from Ovid's *Ex Ponto*.

Something was said in the opening paragraphs of this introduction about Jonson's career. But Renaissance writers often speak of verse as having a career after the poet's death, such 'immortality' being a major theme, for example, in Shakespeare's sonnets. There is, then, a sense in which Jonson's career should include the fate of his work after his death, and, although the history of the reception of his writing from his death up to the present time is too long a story to tell here, it is perhaps appropriate to sketch the reception of Jonson's poems. The first point to make is that the poems have often been seen as only a minor part in the context of the man and his work. More precisely, Jonson's posthumous reputation has often been dominated by comparisons with Shakespeare (usually in Jonson's disfavour, at least in the eighteenth and nineteenth centuries), while his massive and varied output has often been shrunk to two or three of his plays.

Jonson's non-dramatic verse, however, had great influence on English poetry throughout the seventeenth century; and this influence takes various forms. Technically, his development of the couplet (both decasyllabic and octosyllabic) helps that refinement of the form to be seen in Denham, Waller, Cowley and Dryden. The emphasis Jonson gives to social and public verse is reflected in the centrality of such verse in poets like Dryden (again) and Cotton, while the satirical strand in his verse prefigures the ubiquity of satire in Restoration poetry. Similarly, Jonson's powerful tendency to analyse material in ethical terms influences public poetry throughout the century, while his 'plain' style provides a challenging alternative to Spenserian and metaphysical modes. It can also be argued that Jonson's example, mediated by later seventeenth-century poets, bears importantly on the social and satirical manners of the eighteenth.

Although appreciation of Jonson's verse never disappears completely, the English Romanticism of the early nineteenth century created a climate hardly favourable to his type of writing, and much Romantic and post-Romantic comment concentrates on the lack of 'divine afflatus' in his verse, which is seen as creeping and hopping rather than flying. And if Shakespeare was often used to denigrate Jonson, our own century has seen neglect of Jonson's non-dramatic poetry in favour of the verse of John Donne and his 'school'. The concentration on Donne and his school, to be more exact, is a feature of English and American criticism in the first half of the twentieth century, kick-started by Grierson and T. S. Eliot and quite rapidly embraced in university departments of English and in secondary schools. For reasons which cannot be analysed here, however, the past forty years have seen both more good criticism of Jonson's poetry than ever before and renewed recognition that Jonson is as major a figure in English poetry as in drama. This book is a product of these two developments.

A selection such as this one cannot attempt to annotate Jonson's use of the classics in his poetry, which is unfortunate, in that examination of how he uses such material can tell us a lot about his artfulness. Readers who want to study this are referred to the Penguin *Complete Poems*. Jonson's classicism is nothing to be afraid of.

CHRONOLOGY

1572	Born, probably 11 June, probably in London. Father died about one month previously.
	Virtually nothing is known about Jonson's ancestry. Claims in *Conversations* that his paternal grandfather came from Annandale, served Henry VIII and 'was a gentleman'. Same source states father 'turned minister' after suffering loss of his estate under Queen Mary. The striking anecdote about his mother in *Conversations* is all we know of her character.
1574–5	? Mother remarries. Second husband a Westminster bricklayer, of whom nothing useful is known.
1586–8	? At Westminster School through the good offices of a friend, who may, or may not, have been his teacher William Camden.
1588	? Brief, distasteful period at 'another craft', presumably bricklaying.
1591–2	? Short period serving with the army in the Netherlands, possibly followed by more bricklaying.
1594	Marries Anne Lewis, 'a shrew yet honest': little else known.
1597	In Henslowe's employ as actor-writer (probably preceded by a period of acting with a 'strolling company'). Imprisoned for acting in and part-writing the lost play *The Isle of Dogs*.
1598	? Performance of *The Case is Altered* by the Children of the Chapel Royal.
	Every Man in His Humour performed by the Lord Chamberlain's Men.
	Kills the actor Gabriel Spencer in a duel; imprisoned but released by pleading benefit of clergy; converted to Roman Catholicism while in gaol.

1599   *Every Man out of His Humour* performed by the Lord Chamberlain's Men.

1600–1601 *Cynthia's Revels* and *Poetaster* both performed by the Children of the Chapel Royal. Both part of the War of the Theatres (mainly Jonson versus Marston and Dekker).

1601   ? Death of Jonson's first daughter, Mary.

1603   Failure of *Sejanus*, performed by the King's Men. Death of first son, Benjamin, then seven years old.

1605   *Masque of Blackness*, one of Jonson's first court commissions (Jonson wrote fairly regularly for the court for the next twenty-five years or so).

1605–6   *Eastward Ho!* (written with Chapman and Marston) acted by the Children of the Queen's Revels. Jonson and Chapman imprisoned for alleged anti-Scots aspersions in the play.

1606   *Volpone* performed by the King's Men, and also probably at Oxford and Cambridge.

1609   *Epicoene* acted by the Children of the Queen's Revels.

1610   *Alchemist* acted by the King's Men.
         ? Returns to Anglicanism.

1611   *Catiline* (King's Men) fails.

1612–13   In France as tutor to Walter, son of Sir Walter Raleigh.

1614   *Bartholomew Fair* performed by Lady Elizabeth's Men.

1616   *The Devil is an Ass* performed by the King's Men. Publication of folio *Works*, which includes *Epigrams* and *The Forest*. This publication attracted derision as making pretentious claims for the importance of drama but was an important step in furthering recognition of plays as serious writing.
        Granted royal pension.

1618–19	Walks to Scotland and back; meets Drummond in Scotland.
1619	Honorary MA of Oxford.
1623	? Teaches at Gresham College, London. Fire at lodgings destroys books and papers.
1626	*Staple of News* acted by the King's Men.
1628	Made City Chronologer. Paralysed by a stroke.
1629	Failure of *The New Inn* (King's Men).
1631	Beginning of feud with Inigo Jones (though the two men seem to have quarrelled earlier).
1632	*Magnetic Lady* performed by the King's Men.
1633	Revised *Tale of a Tub* acted by Queen Henrietta's Men.
1635	Death of a second son.
1637	Dies in Westminster; buried in Westminster Abbey, 9 August.
1638	Publication of commemorative volume *Jonsonus Virbius*.
1640	Publication of two-volume folio *Works* put out by Sir Kenelm Digby (includes *Underwoods* and *Discoveries*).

EPIGRAMS

To the Reader

Pray thee, take care, that tak'st my book in hand,
To read it well: that is, to understand.

To My Book

It will be looked for, book, when some but see
Thy title, *Epigrams*, and named of me,
Thou should'st be bold, licentious, full of gall,
Wormwood, and sulphur, sharp, and toothed withal;
Become a petulant thing, hurl ink, and wit,
As madmen stones: not caring whom they hit.
Deceive their malice, who could wish it so.
And by thy wiser temper, let men know
Thou are not covetous of least self-fame.
Made from the hazard of another's shame: 10
Much less with lewd, profane, and beastly phrase,
To catch the world's loose laughter, or vain gaze.
He that departs with his own honesty
For vulgar praise, doth it too dearly buy.

To My Bookseller

~

Thou, that mak'st gain thy end, and wisely well,
Call'st a book good, or bad, as it doth sell,
Use mine so, too: I give thee leave. But crave
For the luck's sake, it thus much favour have,
To lie upon thy stall, till it be sought;
Not offered, as it made suit to be bought;
Nor have my title-leaf on posts, or walls,
Or in cleft sticks, advancèd to make calls
For termers, or some clerk-like serving-man,
10   Who scarce can spell the hard names: whose knight
    less can.
If, without these vile arts, it will not sell,
Send it to Bucklersbury, there 'twill, well.

To King James

~

How, best of kings, dost thou a sceptre bear!
How, best of poets, dost thou laurel wear!
But two things, rare, the Fates had in their store,
And gave thee both, to show they could no more.
For such a poet, while thy days were green,
Thou wert, as chief of them are said t'have been.
And such a prince thou art, we daily see,
As chief of those still promise they will be.
Whom should my muse then fly to, but the best
10   Of kings for grace; of poets for my test?

On the Union

∞

When was there contract better driven by Fate?
Or celebrated with more truth of state?
The world the temple was, the priest a king,
The spousèd pair two realms, the sea the ring.

To Alchemists

∞

If all you boast of your great art be true;
Sure, willing poverty lives most in you.

On the New Hot-House

∞

Where lately harboured many a famous whore,
A purging bill, now fixed upon the door,
Tells you it is a hot-house: so it may,
And still be a whore house. They are *synonima*.

On a Robbery

∞

Ridway robbed Duncote of three hundred pound,
Ridway was ta'en, arraigned, condemned to die;
But, for this money was a courtier found,
Begged Ridway's pardon: Duncote, now, doth cry,
Robbed both of money, and the law's relief,
The courtier is become the greater thief.

To All, to Whom I Write

∞

May none, whose scattered names honour my book,
For strict degrees of rank, or title look:
'Tis 'gainst the manners of an epigram:
And, I a poet here, no herald am.

To My Lord Ignorant

∞

Thou call'st me poet, as a term of shame:
But I have my revenge made, in thy name.

On Something, that Walks Somewhere

∞

At court I met it, in clothes brave enough,
To be a courtier; and looks grave enough,
To seem a statesman: as I near it came,
It made me a great face, I asked the name.
A lord, it cried, buried in flesh, and blood,
And such from whom let no man hope least good,
For I will do none: and as little ill,
For I will dare none. Good lord, walk dead still.

On Lieutenant Shift

∞

Shift here, in town, not meanest among squires,
That haunt Pikthatch, Marshlambeth, and Whitefriars,
Keeps himself, with half a man, and defrays
The charge of that state, with this charm, god pays.
By that one spell he lives, eats, drinks, arrays
Himself: his whole revénue is, god pays.
The quarter-day is come; the hostess says,
She must have money: he returns, god pays.
The tailor brings a suit home; he it 'ssays,
Looks o'er the bill, likes it: and says, god pays.   10
He steals to ordinaries; there he plays
At dice his borrowed money: which, god pays.
Then takes up fresh commodity, for days;
Signs to new bond, forfeits: and cries, god pays.
That lost, he keeps his chamber, reads essays,
Takes physic, tears the papers: still god pays.
Or else by water goes, and so to plays;

Calls for his stool, adorns the stage: god pays.
To every cause he meets, this voice he brays:
20   His only answer is to all, god pays.
Not his poor cockatrice but he betrays
Thus: and for his lechery, scores, god pays.
But see! The old bawd hath served him in his trim,
Lent him a pocky whore. She hath paid him.

To Doctor Empiric
∽

When men a dangerous disease did 'scape,
Of old, they gave a cock to Aesculape;
Let me give two; that doubly am got free,
From my disease's danger, and from thee.

To William Camden
∽

Camden, most reverend head, to whom I owe
All that I am in arts, all that I know,
(How nothing's that?) to whom my country owes
The great renown, and name wherewith she goes.
Than thee the age sees not that thing more grave,
More high, more holy, that she more would crave.
What name, what skill, what faith hast thou in things!
What sight in searching the most antique springs!
What weight, and what authority in thy speech!
10   Man scarce can make that doubt, but thou canst teach.
Pardon free truth, and let thy modesty,

18

Which conquers all, be once overcome by thee.
Many of thine this better could, than I,
But for their powers, accept my piety.

On Court-Worm

∽

All men are worms: but this no man. In silk
'Twas brought to court first wrapped, and white as
   milk;
Where, afterwards, it grew a butterfly:
Which was a caterpillar. So 'twill die.

To Brain-Hardy

∽

Hardy, thy brain is valiant, 'tis confessed,
Thou more; that with it every day, dar'st jest
Thyself into fresh brawls: when, called upon,
Scarce thy week's swearing brings thee off, of one.
So, in short time, th'art in arrearage grown
Some hundred quarrels, yet dost thou fight none;
Nor need'st thou: for those few, by oath released,
Make good what thou dar'st do in all the rest.
Keep thyself there, and think thy valour right,
He that dares damn himself, dares more than fight.   10

To the Learnèd Critic

∞

May others fear, fly, and traduce thy name,
As guilty men do magistrates: glad I,
That wish my poems a legitimate fame,
Charge them, for crown, to thy sole censure high.
And, but a sprig of bays, given by thee,
Shall outlive garlands, stol'n from the chaste tree.

To My Mere English Censurer

∞

To thee, my way in epigrams seems new,
When both it is the old way, and the true.
Thou say'st, that cannot be: for thou hast seen
Davies, and Weever, and the best have been,
And mine come nothing like. I hope so. Yet,
As theirs did with thee, mine might credit get:
If thou'ld'st but use thy faith, as thou didst then,
When thou wert wont t'admire, not censure men.
Prithee believe still, and not judge so fast,
10   Thy faith is all the knowledge that thou hast.

On Sir Cod the Perfumed

∞

That Cod can get no widow, yet a knight,
I scent the cause: he woos with an ill sprite.

To the Same Sir Cod

∞

Th'expense in odours is a most vain sin,
Except thou could'st, Sir Cod, wear them within.

On Reformed Gamester

∞

Lord, how is gamester changed! His hair close cut!
His neck fenced round with ruff! His eyes half shut!
His clothes two fashions off, and poor! His sword
Forbid' his side! And nothing, but the Word
Quick in his lips! Who hath this wonder wrought?
The late ta'en bastinado. So I thought.
What several ways men to their calling have!
The body's stripes, I see, the soul may save.

On My First Daughter

∽

Here lies to each her parents' ruth,
Mary, the daughter of their youth:
Yet, all heaven's gifts, being heaven's due,
It makes the father, less, to rue.
At six months' end, she parted hence
With safety of her innocence;
Whose soul heaven's queen, (whose name she bears)
In comfort of her mother's tears,
Hath placed amongst her virgin train:
10   Where, while that severed doth remain,
This grave partakes the fleshly birth.
Which cover lightly, gentle earth.

To John Donne

∽

Donne, the delight of Phoebus, and each muse,
Who, to thy one, all other brains refuse;
Whose every work, of thy most early wit,
Came forth example, and remains so, yet:
Longer a–knowing, than most wits do live,
And which no affection praise enough can give!
To it, thy language, letters, arts, best life,
Which might with half mankind maintain a strife.
All which I meant to praise, and, yet, I would;
10   But leave, because I cannot as I should!

To the Parliament

∾

There's reason good, that you good laws should make:
Men's manners ne'er were viler, for your sake.

On Sir Voluptuous Beast

∾

While Beast instructs his fair, and innocent wife,
In the past pleasures of his sensual life,
Telling the motions of each petticoat,
And how his Ganymede moved, and how his goat,
And now, her (hourly) her own cucqueen makes,
In varied shapes, which for his lust she takes:
What doth he else, but say, leave to be chaste,
Just wife, and, to change me, make woman's haste.

On the Same Beast

∾

Than his chaste wife, though Beast now know no more,
He adulters still: his thoughts lie with a whore.

On Sir John Roe

In place of scutcheons, that should deck thy hearse,
Take better ornaments, my tears, and verse.
If any sword could save from Fates, Roe's could;
If any muse outlive their spite, his can;
If any friend's tears could restore, his would;
If any pious life e'er lifted man
To heaven, his hath: O happy state! wherein
We, sad for him, may glory, and not sin.

On Don Surly

Don Surly, to aspire the glorious name
Of a great man, and to be thought the same,
Makes serious use of all great trade he knows.
He speaks to men with a rhinocerote's nose,
Which he thinks great; and so reads verses, too;
And, that is done, as he saw great men do.
H'has tympanies of business, in his face,
And, can forget men's names, with a great grace.
He will both argue, and discourse in oaths,
Both which are great. And laugh at ill-made clothes;
That's greater, yet: to cry his own up neat.
He doth, at meals, alone, his pheasant eat,
Which is main greatness. And, at his still board,
He drinks to no man: that's too, like a lord.
He keeps another's wife, which is a spice
Of solemn greatness. And he dares, at dice,
Blaspheme God, greatly. Or some poor hind beat,

That breathes in his dog's way: and this is great.
Nay more, for greatness' sake, he will be one
May hear my epigrams, but like of none.   20
Surly, use other arts, these only can
Style thee a most great fool, but no great man.

To Sir Annual Tilter

∞

Tilter, the most may admire thee, though not I:
And thou, right guiltless, mayst plead to it, why?
For thy late sharp device. I say 'tis fit
All brains, at times of triumph, should run wit.
For then, our water-conduits do run wine;
But that's put in, thou'lt say. Why, so is thine.

To Person Guilty

∞

Guilty, be wise; and though thou know'st the crimes
Be thine, I tax, yet do not own my rhymes:
'Twere madness in thee, to betray thy fame,
And person to the world; ere I thy name.

On Sir John Roe

What two brave perils of the private sword
Could not effect, not all the furies do,
That self-divided Belgia did afford;
What not the envy of the seas reached to,
The cold of Moscow, and fat Irish air,
His often change of clime (though not of mind)
What could not work; at home in his repair
Was his blessed fate, but our hard lot to find.
Which shows, wherever death doth please t'appear,
10   Seas, serenes, swords, shot, sickness, all are there.

To the Same

I'll not offend thee with a vain tear more,
Glad-mentioned Roe: thou art but gone before,
Whither the world must follow. And I, now,
Breathe to expect my when, and make my how.
Which if most gracious heaven grant like thine,
Who wets my grave, can be no friend of mine.

Of Death

He that fears death, or mourns it, in the just,
Shows of the resurrection little trust.

To King James

∽

Who would not be thy subject, James, t'obey
A prince, that rules by example, more than sway?
Whose manners draw, more than thy powers constrain.
And in this short time of thy happiest reign,
Hast purged thy realms, as we have now no cause
Left us of fear, but first our crimes, then laws.
Like aids 'gainst treasons who hath found before?
And than in them, how could we know God more?
First thou preservèd wert, our king to be,
And since, the whole land was preserved for thee.　　　10

On Cheveril the Lawyer

∽

No cause, nor client fat, will Cheveril leese,
But as they come, on both sides he takes fees,
And pleaseth both. For while he melts his grease
For this: that wins, for whom he holds his peace.

To Robert, Earl of Salisbury

∞

What need hast thou of me, or of my muse,
Whose actions so themselves do celebrate?
Which should thy country's love to speak refuse,
Her foes enough would fame thee in their hate.
'Tofore, great men were glad of poets: now,
I, not the worst, am covetous of thee.
Yet dare not, to my thought, least hope allow
Of adding to thy fame; thine may to me,
When in my book, men read but Cecil's name,
10   And what I write thereof find far, and free
From servile flattery (common poets' shame)
As thou stand'st clear of the necessity.

On My First Son

∞

Farewell, thou child of my right hand, and joy;
My sin was too much hope of thee, loved boy,
Seven years thou wert lent to me, and I thee pay,
Exacted by thy fate, on the just day.
O, could I lose all father, now. For why
Will man lament the state he should envy?
To have so soon 'scaped world's, and flesh's rage,
And, if no other misery, yet age!
Rest in soft peace, and, asked, say here doth lie
10   Ben Jonson his best piece of poetry.
For whose sake, henceforth, all his vows be such,
As what he loves may never like too much.

To Playwright

Playwright me reads, and still my verses damns,
He says, I want the tongue of epigrams;
I have no salt: no bawdry he doth mean.
For witty, in his language, is obscene.
Playwright, I loathe to have thy manners known
In my chaste book: profess them in thine own.

To King James

(UPON THE HAPPY FALSE RUMOUR OF HIS DEATH,
THE TWO AND TWENTIETH DAY OF MARCH, 1607)
That we the loss might know, and thou our love,
Great heaven did well, to give ill fame free wing;
Which though it did but panic terror prove,
And far beneath least pause of such a king,
Yet give thy jealous subjects leave to doubt:
Who this thy 'scape from rumour gratulate,
No less than if from peril; and devout,
Do beg thy care unto thy after-state.
For we, that have our eyes still in our ears,
Look not upon thy dangers, but our fears.   10

To Censorious Courtling

∞

Courtling, I rather thou shouldst utterly
Dispraise my work, than praise it frostily;
When I am read, thou feign'st a weak applause,
As if thou wert my friend, but lackd'st a cause.
This but thy judgement fools: the other way
Would both thy folly, and thy spite betray.

To Francis Beaumont

∞

How I do love thee Beaumont, and thy muse,
That unto me dost such religion use!
How I do fear myself, that am not worth
The least indulgent thought thy pen drops forth!
At once thou mak'st me happy, and unmak'st;
And giving largely to me, more thou tak'st.
What fate is mine, that so itself bereaves?
What art is thine, that so thy friend deceives?
When even there, where most thou praisest me,
10   For writing better, I must envy thee.

On Poet-Ape

Poor Poet-Ape, that would be thought our chief,
Whose works are e'en the frippery of wit,
From brocage is become so bold a thief,
As we, the robbed, leave rage, and pity it.
At first he made low shifts, would pick and glean,
Buy the reversion of old plays; now grown
To a little wealth, and credit in the scene,
He takes up all, makes each man's wit his own.
And, told of this, he slights it. Tut, such crimes
The sluggish gaping auditor devours;   10
He marks not whose 'twas first: and after-times
May judge it to be his, as well as ours.
Fool, as if half-eyes will not know a fleece
From locks of wool, or shreds from the whole piece!

On Spies

Spies, you are lights in state, but of base stuff,
Who, when you have burnt yourselves down to the snuff,
Stink, and are thrown away. End fair enough.

To Fine Lady Would-Be

∞

Fine Madam Would-be, wherefore should you fear,
That love to make so well, a child to bear?
The world reputes you barren: but I know
Your 'pothecary, and his drug says no.
Is it the pain affrights? That's soon forgot.
Or your complexion's loss? You have a pot,
That can restore that. Will it hurt your feature?
To make amends, you're thought a wholesome
    creature.
What should the cause be? Oh, you live at court:
10   And there's both loss of time, and loss of sport
In a great belly. Write, then on thy womb,
Of the not born, yet buried, here's the tomb.

To Robert, Earl of Salisbury

∞

Who can consider thy right courses run,
With what thy virtue on the times hath won,
And not thy fortune; who can clearly see
The judgement of the king so shine in thee;
And that thou seek'st reward of thy each act,
Not from the public voice, but private fact;
Who can behold all envy so declined
By constant suffering of thy equal mind;
And can to these be silent, Salisbury,
10   Without his, thine, and all times' injury?
Cursed be his muse, that could lie dumb, or hid
To so true worth, though thou thyself forbid.

To My Muse
∞

Away and leave me, thou thing most abhorred
That hast betrayed me to a worthless lord;
Made me commit most fierce idolatry
To a great image through thy luxury.
Be thy next master's more unlucky muse,
And, as thou hast mine, his hours, and youth abuse.
Get him the time's long grudge, the court's ill will;
And, reconciled, keep him suspected still.
Make him lose all his friends; and, which is worse,
Almost all ways, to any better course.   10
With me thou leav'st an happier muse than thee,
And which thou brought'st me, welcome poverty.

To Thomas, Earl of Suffolk
∞

Since men have left to do praiseworthy things,
Most think all praises flatteries. But truth brings
That sound, and that authority with her name,
As, to be raised by her, is only fame.
Stand high, then, Howard, high in eyes of men,
High in thy blood, thy place, but highest then,
When, in men's wishes, so thy virtues wrought,
As all thy honours were by them first sought:
And thou designed to be the same thou art,
Before thou wert it, in each good man's heart.   10
Which, by no less confirmed, than thy king's choice,
Proves, that is God's which was the people's voice.

To Thomas, Lord Chancellor

∽

Whilst thy weighed judgments, Egerton, I hear,
And know thee, then, a judge, not of one year;
Whilst I behold thee live with purest hands;
That no affection in thy voice commands;
That still th'art present to the better cause;
And no less wise, than skilful in the laws;
Whilst thou art certain to thy words, once gone,
As is thy conscience, which is always one:
The virgin, long since fled from earth, I see,
10 T'our times returned, hath made her heaven in thee.

On Lip the Teacher

∽

I cannot think there's that antipathy
'Twixt puritans, and players, as some cry;
Though Lip, at Paul's, ran from his text away,
T'inveigh 'gainst players: what did he then but play?

On Lucy, Countess of Bedford

∽

This morning, timely rapt with holy fire,
I thought to form unto my zealous muse,
What kind of creature I could most desire,
To honour, serve, and love; as poets use.
I meant to make her fair, and free, and wise,
Of greatest blood, and yet more good than great;
I meant the day-star should not brighter rise,
Nor lend like influence from his lucent seat.
I meant she should be courteous, facile, sweet,
Hating that solemn vice of greatness, pride;   10
I meant each softest virtue, there should meet,
Fit in that softer bosom to reside.
Only a learnèd, and a manly soul
I purposed her; that should, with even powers,
The rock, the spindle, and the shears control
Of destiny, and spin her own free hours.
Such when I meant to feign, and wished to see,
My muse bad, *Bedford* write, and that was she.

Of Life and Death

∽

The ports of death are sins; of life, good deeds:
Through which, our merit leads us to our meeds.
How wilful blind is he then, that would stray,
And hath it, in his powers, to make his way!
This world death's region is, the other life's:
And here, it should be one of our first strifes,
So to front death, as men might judge us past it.
For good men but see death, the wicked taste it.

To Lucy, Countess of Bedford

∞

Madam, I told you late how I repented,
I asked a lord a buck, and he denied me;
And, ere I could ask you, I was prevented:
For your most noble offer had supplied me.
Straight went I home; and there most like a poet,
I fancied to myself, what wine, what wit
I would have spent: how every muse should know it,
And Phoebus' self should be at eating it.
O madam, if your grant did thus transfer me,
10 Make it your gift. See whither that will bear me.

On Captain Hazard the Cheater

∞

Touched with the sin of false play, in his punk,
Hazard a month forswore his; and grew drunk,
Each night, to drown his cares: but when the gain
Of what she had wrought came in, and waked his brain,
Upon the account, hers grew the quicker trade.
Since when he's sober again, and all play's made.

To Edward Alleyn

∽

If Rome so great, and in her wisest age,
Feared not to boast the glories of her stage,
As skilful Roscius, and grave Aesop, men,
Yet crowned with honours, as with riches, then;
Who had no less a trumpet of their name,
Than Cicero, whose every breath was fame:
How can so great example die in me,
That, Alleyn, I should pause to publish thee?
Who both their graces in thyself hast more
Outstripped, than they did all that went before: 10
And present worth in all dost so contract,
As others speak, but only thou dost act.
Wear this renown. 'Tis just, that who did give
So many poets life, by one should live.

On Mill, My Lady's Woman

∽

When Mill first came to court, the unprofiting fool,
Unworthy such a mistress, such a school,
Was dull, and long, ere she would go to man:
At last, ease, appetite, and example wan
The nicer thing to taste her lady's page;
And, finding good security in his age,
Went on: and proving him still, day by day,
Discerned no difference of his years, or play.
Not though that hair grew brown, which once was amber,
And he grown youth, was called to his lady's chamber,   10
Still Mill continued: nay, his face growing worse,

And he removed to gent'man of the horse,
Mill was the same. Since, both his body and face
Blown up; and he (too unwieldy for that place)
Hath got the steward's chair; he will not tarry
Longer a day, but with his Mill will marry.
And it is hoped, that she, like Milo, wull
First bearing him a calf, bear him a bull.

To Sir Horace Vere

∽

Which of thy names I take, not only bears
A Roman sound, but Roman virtue wears,
Illustrious Vere, or Horace; fit to be
Sung by a Horace, or a muse as free;
Which thou art to thyself: whose fame was won
In the eye of Europe, where thy deeds were done,
When on thy trumpet she did sound a blast,
Whose relish to eternity shall last.
I leave thy acts, which should I prosecute
10 Throughout, might flattery seem; and to be mute
To any one, were envy: which would live
Against my grave, and time could not forgive.
I speak thy other graces, not less shown,
Nor less in practice; but less marked, less known:
Humanity, and piety, which are
As noble in great chiefs, as they are rare.
And best become the valiant man to wear,
Who more should seek men's reverence, than fear.

To Sir Thomas Roe

∞

Thou hast begun well, Roe, which stand well too,
And I know nothing more thou hast to do.
He that is round within himself, and straight,
Need seek no other strength, no other height;
Fortune upon him breaks herself, if ill,
And what would hurt his virtue makes it still.
That thou at once, then, nobly may'st defend
With thine own course the judgement of thy friend,
Be always to thy gathered self the same:
And study conscience, more than thou wouldst fame.   10
Though both be good, the latter yet is worst,
And ever is ill got without the first.

To the Same

∞

That thou hast kept thy love, increased thy will,
Bettered thy trust to letters; that thy skill;
Hast taught thyself worthy thy pen to tread,
And that to write things worthy to be read:
How much of great example wert thou, Roe,
If time to facts, as unto men would owe?
But much it now avails, what's done, of whom:
The selfsame deeds, as diversely they come,
From place, or fortune, are made high, or low,
And even the praiser's judgement suffers so.   10
Well, though thy name less than our great ones' be,
Thy fact is more: let truth encourage thee.

Inviting a Friend to Supper

Tonight, grave sir, both my poor house, and I
Do equally desire your company:
Not that we think us worthy such a guest,
But that your worth will dignify our feast,
With those that come; whose grace may make that
    seem
Something, which, else, could hope for no esteem.
It is the fair acceptance, sir, creates
The entertainment perfect: not the cates.
Yet shall you have, to rectify your palate,
10 An olive, capers, or some better salad
Ush'ring the mutton; with a short-legged hen,
If we can get her, full of eggs, and then,
Lemons, and wine for sauce: to these, a cony
Is not to be despaired of, for our money;
And, though fowl, now, be scarce, yet there are clerks,
The sky not falling, think we may have larks.
I'll tell you of more, and lie, so you will come:
Of partridge, pheasant, woodcock, of which some
May yet be there; and godwit, if we can:
20 Knat, rail, and ruff too. Howsoe'er, my man
Shall read a piece of Virgil, Tacitus,
    Livy, or of some better book to us,
Of which we'll speak our minds, amidst our meat;
And I'll profess no verses to repeat:
To this, if aught appear, which I not know of,
That will the pastry, not my paper, show of.
Digestive cheese, and fruit there sure will be;
But that, which most doth take my muse, and me,
Is a pure cup of rich canary wine,
30 Which is the Mermaid's, now, but shall be mine:
Of which had Horace, or Anacreon tasted,
Their lives, as do their lines, till now had lasted.

Tobacco, nectar, or the Thespian spring,
Are all but Luther's beer, to this I sing.
Of this we will sup free, but moderately,
And we will have no Pooly, or Parrot by;
Nor shall our cups make any guilty men:
But, at our parting, we will be, as when
We innocently met. No simple word,
That shall be uttered at our mirthful board,   40
Shall make us sad next morning: or affright
The liberty, that we'll enjoy tonight.

To Mary, Lady Wroth

∽

How well, fair crown of your fair sex, might he,
That but the twilight of your sprite did see,
And noted for what flesh such souls were framed,
Know you to be a Sidney, though unnamed?
And, being named, how little doth that name
Need any muse's praise to give it fame?
Which is, itself, the imprese of the great,
And glory of them all, but to repeat!
Forgive me then, if mine but say you are
A Sidney: but in that extend as far   10
As loudest praisers, who perhaps would find
For every part a character assigned.
My praise is plain, and wheresoe'er professed,
Becomes none more than you, who need it least.

To Mary, Lady Wroth

∽

Madam, had all antiquity been lost,
All history sealed up, and fables crossed;
That we had left us, nor by time, nor place,
Least mention of a nymph, a muse, a grace,
But even their names were to be made anew,
Who could not but create them all, from you?
He, that but saw you wear the wheaten hat,
Would call you more than Ceres, if not that:
And, dressed in shepherd's 'tire, who would not say:
You were the bright Oenone, Flora, or May?
If dancing, all would cry the Idalian queen,
Were leading forth the graces on the green:
And armèd to the chase, so bare her bow
Diana alone, so hit, and hunted so.
There's none so dull, that for your stile would ask,
That saw you put on Pallas' pluméd casque:
Or, keeping your due state, that would not cry,
There Juno sat, and yet no peacock by.
So are you Nature's index, and restore,
In yourself, all treasure lost of th'age before.

To True Soldiers

∽

Strength of my country, whilst I bring to view
Such as are miscalled captains, and wrong you;
And your high names: I do desire, that thence
Be nor put on you, nor you take offence.

42

I swear by your true friend, my muse, I love
Your great profession; which I once did prove:
And did not shame it with my actions, then,
No more, than I dare now do, with my pen.
He that not trusts me, having vowed thus much,
But's angry for the captain, still: is such.　　　10

To a Weak Gamester in Poetry

∽

With thy small stock, why are thou vent'ring still,
At this so subtle sport: and play'st so ill?
Think'st thou it is mere fortune, that can win?
Or thy rank setting? That thou dar'st put in
Thy all, at all: and whatsoe'er I do,
Art still at that, and think'st to blow me up too?
I cannot for the stage a drama lay,
Tragic, or comic; but thou writ'st the play.
I leave thee there, and giving way, intend
An epic poem; thou hast the same end.　　　10
I modestly quit that, and think to write,
Next morn, an ode: thou mak'st a song ere night.
I pass to elegies; thou meet'st me there:
To satires; and thou dost pursue me. Where,
Where shall I 'scape thee? In an epigram?
O (thou cry'st out) that is thy proper game.
Troth, if it be, I pity thy ill luck;
That both for wit, and sense, so oft dost pluck,
And never art encountered, I confess:
Nor scarce dost colour for it, which is less.　　　20
Prithee, yet save thy rest; give o'er in time:
There's no vexation, that can make thee prime.

To Mrs Philip Sidney

I must believe some miracles still be,
When Sidney's name I hear, or face I see:
For Cupid, who (at first) took vain delight,
In mere out-forms, until he lost his sight,
Hath changed his soul, and made his object you:
Where finding so much beauty met with virtue,
He hath not only gained himself his eyes,
But, in your love, made all his servants wise.

On Gut

Gut eats all day, and lechers all the night,
So all his meat he tasteth over, twice:
And, striving so to double his delight,
He makes himself a thoroughfare of vice.
Thus, in his belly, can he change a sin,
Lust it comes out, that gluttony went in.

Epitaph on S.P., a Child of Q[ueen] El[izabeth's] Chapel

∽

Weep with me all you that read
   This little story:
And know, for whom a tear you shed,
   Death's self is sorry.
'Twas a child, that so did thrive
   In grace, and feature,
As Heaven and Nature seemed to strive
   Which owned the creature.
Years he numbered scarce thirteen
   When Fates turned cruel,   10
Yet three filled zodiacs had he been
   The stage's jewel;
And did act (what now we moan)
   Old men so duly,
As, sooth, the Parcae thought him one,
   He played so truly.
So, by error, to his fate
   They all consented;
But viewing him since (alas, too late)
   They have repented.   20
And have sought (to give new birth)
   In baths to steep him;
But, being so much too good for earth,
   Heaven vows to keep him.

Epitaph on Elizabeth, L.H.

∞

Wouldst thou hear, what man can say
In a little? Reader, stay.
Underneath this stone doth lie
As much beauty, as could die:
Which in life did harbour give
To more virtue, than doth live.
If, at all, she had a fault,
Leave it buried in this vault.
One name was Elizabeth,
10   The other let it sleep with death:
Fitter, where it died, to tell,
Than that it lived at all. Farewell.

On the Famous Voyage

∞

No more let Greece her bolder fables tell
Of Hercules, or Theseus going to hell,
Orpheus, Ulysses: or the Latin muse,
With tales of Troy's just knight, our faiths abuse:
We have a Shelton, and a Heyden got,
Had power to act, what they to feign had not.
All, that they boast of Styx, of Acheron,
Cocytus, Phlegeton, our have proved in one;
The filth, stench, noise: save only what was there
10   Subtly distinguished, was confusèd here.
Their wherry had no sail, too; ours had none:
And in it, two more horrid knaves than Charon.
Arses were heard to croak, instead of frogs;

46

And for one Cerberus, the whole coast was dogs.
Furies there wanted not: each scold was ten.
And, for the cries of ghosts, women, and men,
Laden with plague-sores, and their sins, were heard,
Lashed by their consciences, to die, afeared.
Then let the former age, with this content her,
She brought the poets forth, but ours the adventer. 20

THE VOYAGE ITSELF

I sing the brave adventure of two wights,
And pity 'tis, I cannot call them knights:
One was; and he, for brawn, and brain, right able
To have been stylèd of King Arthur's table.
The other was a squire, of fair degree;
But, in the action, greater man than he:
Who gave, to take at his return from Hell,
His three for one. Now, lordings, listen well.
    It was the day, what time the powerful moon
Makes the poor Bankside creature wet it' shoon, 30
In its own hall; when these (in worthy scorn
Of those, that put out monies, on return
From Venice, Paris, or some inland passage
Of six times to, and fro, without embassage,
Or him that backward went to Berwick, or which
Did dance the famous Morris, unto Norwich)
At Bread Street's Mermaid, having dined, and merry,
Proposed to go to Holborn in a wherry:
A harder task, than either his to Bristo',
Or his to Antwerp. Therefore, once more list ho. 40
    A dock there is, that called is Avernus,
Of some Bridewell, and may, in time, concern us
All, that are readers: but, methinks 'tis odd,
That all this while I have forgot some god,
Or goddess to invoke, to stuff my verse;
And with both bombard style, and phrase, rehearse
The many perils of this port, and how
Sans help of Sybil, or a golden bough,
Or magic sacrifice, they passed along!

50 Alcides, be thou succouring to my song.
   'Thou hast seen hell (some say) and know'st all nooks
     there,
   Canst tell me best, how every Fury looks there,
   And art a god, if Fame thee not abuses,
   Always at hand, to aid the merry muses.
   Great club-fist, though thy back, and bones be sore,
   Still, with thy former labours; yet, once more,
   Act a brave work, call it thy last adventry:
   But hold my torch, while I describe the entry
   To this dire passage. Say, thou stop thy nose:
60 'Tis but light pains: indeed this dock's no rose.

    In the first jaws appeared that ugly monster,
   Ycleped Mud, which, when their oars did once stir,
   Belched forth an air, as hot, as at the muster
   Of all your night-tubs, when the carts do cluster,
   Who shall discharge first his merd-urinous load:
   Thorough her womb they make their famous road,
   Between two walls; where, on one side, to scar men,
   Were seen your ugly centaurs, ye call car-men,
   Gorgonian scolds, and harpies: on the other
70 Hung stench, diseases, and old filth, their mother,
   With famine, wants, and sorrows many a dozen,
   The least of which was to the plague a cousin.
   But they unfrighted pass, though many a privy
   Spake to them louder, than the ox in Livy;
   And many a sink poured out her rage anenst 'hem;
   But still their valour, and their virtue fenced 'hem,
   And, on they went, like Castor brave, and Pollux:
   Ploughing the main. When see (the worst of all lucks)
   They met the second prodigy, would fear a
80 Man, that had never heard of a Chimera.
   One said, it was bold Briareus, or the beadle,
   (Who hath the hundred hands when he doth meddle)
   The other thought it Hydra, or the rock
   Made of the trull, that cut her father's lock:
   But, coming near, they found it but a lighter,
   So huge, it seemed, they could by no means quit her.

'Back', cried their brace of Charons: they cried, 'No,
No going back; on still you rogues, and row.
How hight the place?' A voice was heard, 'Cocytus.'
'Row close then, slaves.' 'Alas, they will beshite us.' 90
'No matter, stinkards, row. What croaking sound
Is this we hear? Of frogs?' 'No, guts wind-bound,
Over your heads': 'Well, row.' At this a loud
Crack did report itself, as if a cloud
Had burst with storm, and down fell, *ab excelsis*,
Poor Mercury, crying out on Paracelsus,
And all his followers, that had so abused him:
And, in so shitten sort, so long had used him:
For (where he was the god of eloquence,
And subtlety of metals) they dispense   100
His spirits, now, in pills, and eke in potions,
Suppositories, cataplasms, and lotions.
But many moons there shall not wane (quoth he)
(In the meantime, let them imprison me)
But I will speak (and know I shall be heard)
Touching this cause, where they will be afeared
To answer me. And sure, it was the intent
Of the grave fart, late let in parliament,
Had it been seconded, and not in fume
Vanished away: as you must all presume   110
Their Mercury did now. By this the stem
Of the hulk touched, and, as by Polypheme
The sly Ulysses stole in a sheepskin,
The well-greased wherry now had got between,
And bad her farewell sough, unto the lurden:
Never did bottom more betray her burden;
The meat-boat of Bears' college, Paris garden,
Stunk not so ill; nor, when she kissed, Kate Arden.
Yet, one day in the year, for sweet 'tis voiced,
And that is when it is the Lord Mayor's foist.   120
   By this time had they reached the Stygian pool,
By which the masters swear, when, on the stool
Of worship, they their nodding chins do hit
Against their breasts. Here, several ghosts did flit

49

About the shore, of farts, but late departed,
White, black, blue, green, and in more forms
   outstarted,
Than all those *atomi* ridiculous,
Whereof old Democrite, and Hill Nicholas,
One said, the other swore, the world consists.

130   These be the cause of those thick frequent mists
Arising in that place, through which, who goes,
Must try the unused valour of a nose:
And that ours did. For, yet, no nare was tainted,
Nor thumb, nor finger to the stop acquainted,
But open, and unarmed encountered all:
Whether it languishing stuck upon the wall,
Or were precipitated down the jakes,
And, after, swom abroad in ample flakes,
Or, that it lay, heaped like an usurer's mass,

140   All was to them the same, they were to pass,
And so they did, from Styx, to Acheron:
The ever-boiling flood. Whose banks upon
Your Fleet Lane Furies; and hot cooks do dwell,
That, with still-scalding steams, make the place hell.
The sinks ran grease, and hair of measled hogs,
The heads, houghs, entrails, and the hides of dogs:
For, to say truth, what scullion is so nasty,
To put the skins, and offal in a pasty?
Cats there lay divers had been flayed and roasted,

150   And, after mouldy grown, again were toasted,
Then, selling not, a dish was ta'en to mince them,
But still, it seemed, the rankness did convince them.
For, here they were thrown in with the melted pewter,
Yet drowned they not. They had five lives in future.
   But 'mongst these Tiberts, who do you think there
     was?
Old Banks the juggler, our Pythagoras,
Grave tutor to the learnéd horse. Both which,
Being, beyond sea, burnéd for one witch:
Their spirits transmigrated to a cat:

160   And, now, above the pool, a face right fat

With great grey eyes, are lifted up, and mewed;
Thrice did it spit; thrice dived. At last, it viewed
Our brave heroes with a milder glare,
And, in a piteous tune, began. 'How dare
Your dainty nostrils (in so hot a season,
When every clerk eats artichokes, and peason,
Laxative lettuce, and such windy meat)
'Tempt such a passage? When each privy's seat
Is filled with buttock? And the walls do sweat
Urine, and plasters? When the noise doth beat   170
Upon your ears, of discords so unsweet?
And outcries of the damnéd in the Fleet?
Cannot the plague-bill keep you back? Nor bells
Of loud sepúlchres with their hourly knells,
But you will visit grisly Pluto's hall?
Behold where Cerberus, reared on the wall
Of Holborn (three sergeants' heads) looks o'er,
And stays but till you come unto the door!
Tempt not his fury, Pluto is away:
And madam Caesar, great Proserpina,   180
Is now from home. You lose your labours quite,
Were you Jove's sons, or had Alcides' might'.
They cried out puss. He told them he was Banks,
That had, so often, showed them merry pranks.
They laughed, at his laugh-worthy fate. And passed
The triple head without a sop. At last,
Calling for Radamanthus, that dwelt by,
A soap-boiler; and Aeacus him nigh,
Who kept an ale-house; with my little Minos,
An ancient purblind fletcher, with a high nose;   190
They took them all to witness of their action:
And so went bravely back, without protraction.
    In memory of which most liquid deed,
The city since hath raised a pyramid.
And I could wish for their eternized sakes,
My muse had ploughed with his, that sung A-JAX.

THE FOREST

Why I Write Not of Love

Some act of Love's bound to rehearse,
I thought to bind him, in my verse:
Which when he felt, Away (quoth he)
Can poets hope to fetter me?
It is enough, they once did get
Mars, and my mother, in their net:
I wear not these my wings in vain.
With which he fled me: and again,
Into my rhymes could ne'er be got
10   By any art. Then wonder not,
That since, my numbers are so cold,
When Love is fled, and I grow old.

To Penshurst

Thou art not, Penshurst, built to envious show,
Of touch, or marble; nor canst boast a row
Of polished pillars, or a roof of gold:
Thou hast no lanthern, whereof tales are told;
Or stair, or courts; but stand'st an ancient pile,
And these grudged at, art reverenced the while.

Thou joy'st in better marks, of soil, of air,
Of wood, of water: therein thou art fair.
Thou hast thy walks for health, as well as sport:
Thy Mount, to which the dryads do resort,⁣ 10
Where Pan, and Bacchus their high feasts have made,
Beneath the broad beech, and the chestnut shade;
That taller tree, which of a nut was set,
At his great birth, where all the muses met.
There, in the writhèd bark, are cut the names
Of many a Sylvan, taken with his flames.
And thence, the ruddy satyrs oft provoke
The lighter fauns, to reach thy lady's oak.
Thy copse, too, named of Gamage, thou hast there,
That never fails to serve thee seasoned deer,⁣ 20
When thou would'st feast, or exercise thy friends.
The lower land, that to the river bends,
Thy sheep, thy bullocks, kine, and calves do feed:
The middle grounds thy mares, and horses breed.
Each bank doth yield thee conies; and the tops
Fertile of wood, Ashore, and Sidney's copse,
To crown thy open table, doth provide
The purpled pheasant, with the speckled side:
The painted partridge lies in every field,
And, for thy mess, is willing to be killed.⁣ 30
And if the high-swoll'n Medway fail thy dish,
Thou hast thy ponds, that pay thee tribute fish,
Fat, agéd carps, that run into thy net.
And pikes, now weary their own kind to eat,
As loth, the second draught, or cast to stay,
Officiously, at first, themselves betray.
Bright eels, that emulate them, and leap on land,
Before the fisher, or into his hand.
Then hath thy orchard fruit, thy garden flowers,
Fresh as the air, and new as are the hours.⁣ 40
The early cherry, with the later plum,
Fig, grape, and quince, each in his time doth come:
The blushing apricot, and woolly peach
Hang on thy walls, that every child may reach.

And though thy walls be of the country stone,
They are reared with no man's ruin, no man's groan,
There's none, that dwell about them, wish them down;
But all come in, the farmer, and the clown:
And no one empty-handed, to salute
50 Thy lord, and lady, though they have no suit.
Some bring a capon, some a rural cake,
Some nuts, some apples; some that think they make
The better cheeses, bring them; or else send
By their ripe daughters, whom they would commend
This way to husbands; and whose baskets bear
An emblem of themselves, in plum, or pear.
But what can this (more than express their love)
Add to thy free provisions, far above
The need of such? Whose liberal board doth flow,
60 With all, that hospitality doth know!
Where comes no guest, but is allowed to eat,
Without his fear, and of thy lord's own meat:
Where the same beer, and bread, and self-same wine,
That is his lordship's, shall be also mine.
And I not fain to sit (as some, this day,
At great men's tables) and yet dine away.
Here no man tells my cups; nor, standing by,
A waiter, doth my gluttony envy;
But gives me what I call, and lets me eat,
70 He knows, below, he shall find plenty of meat.
Thy tables hoard not up for the next day,
Nor, when I take my lodging, need I pray
For fire, or lights, or livery: all is there;
As if thou, then, wert mine, or I reigned here:
There's nothing I can wish, for which I stay.
That found King James, when hunting late, this way,
With his brave son, the prince, they saw thy fires
Shine bright on every hearth as the desires
Of thy Penates had been set on flame,
80 To entertain them; or the country came,
With all their zeal, to warm their welcome here.
What (great, I will not say, but) sudden cheer

Didst thou, then, make them! And what praise was heaped
On thy good lady, then! Who, therein, reaped
The just reward of her high huswifery;
To have her linen, plate, and all things nigh,
When she was far: and not a room, but dressed,
As if it had expected such a guest!
These, Penshurst, are thy praise, and yet not all.
Thy lady's noble, fruitful, chaste withal.   90
His children thy great lord may call his own:
A fortune, in this age, but rarely known.
They are, and have been taught religion: thence
Their gentler spirits have sucked innocence.
Each morn, and even, they are taught to pray,
With the whole household, and may, every day,
Read, in their virtuous parents' noble parts,
The mysteries of manners, arms, and arts.
Now, Penshurst, they that will proportion thee
With other edifices, when they see   100
Those proud, ambitious heaps, and nothing else,
May say, their lords have built, but thy lord dwells.

To Sir Robert Wroth

∽

How blessed art thou, canst love the country, Wroth,
    Whether by choice, or fate, or both;
And, though so near the city, and the court,
    Art ta'en with neither's vice, nor sport:
That at great times, art no ambitious guest
    Of sheriff's dinner, or mayor's feast.
Nor com'st to view the better cloth of state;
    The richer hangings, or crown plate;
Nor throng'st (when masquing is) to have a sight
    Of the short bravery of the night;   10

To view the jewels, stuffs, the pains, the wit
    There wasted, some not paid for yet!
But canst, at home, in thy securer rest,
    Live, with unbought provision blessed;
Free from proud porches, or their gilded roofs,
    'Mongst lowing herds, and solid hoofs:
Alongst the curléd woods, and painted meads,
    Through which a serpent river leads
To some cool, courteous shade, which he calls his,
20   And makes sleep softer than it is!
Or, if thou list the night in watch to break,
    Abed canst hear the loud stag speak,
In spring, oft rouséd for thy master's sport,
    Who, for it, makes thy house his court;
Or with thy friends, the heart of all the year,
    Divid'st, upon the lesser deer;
In autumn, at the partridge makes a flight,
    And giv'st thy gladder guests the sight;
And, in the winter, hunt'st the flying hare,
30   More for thy exercise, than fare;
While all, that follow, their glad ears apply
    To the full greatness of the cry:
Or hawking at the river, or the bush,
    Or shooting at the greedy thrush,
Thou dost with some delight the day outwear,
    Although the coldest of the year!
The whilst, the several seasons thou hast seen
    Of flowery fields, of copses green,
The mowèd meadows with the fleecèd sheep,
40   And feasts that either shearers keep;
The ripened ears, yet humble in their height,
    And furrows laden with their weight;
The apple harvest, that doth longer last;
    The hogs returned home fat from mast;
The trees cut out in log; and those boughs made
    A fire now, that lent a shade!
Thus Pan, and Sylvan, having had their rites,
    Comus puts in, for new delights;

And fills thy open hall with mirth, and cheer,
    As if in Saturn's reign it were;   50
Apollo's harp, and Hermes' lyre resound,
    Nor are the muses strangers found:
The rout of rural folk come thronging in,
    (Their rudeness then is thought no sin)
Thy noblest spouse affords them welcome grace;
    And the great heroes, of her race,
Sit mixed with loss of state, or reverence.
    Freedom doth with degree dispense.
The jolly wassail walks the often round,
    And in their cups, their cares are drowned: 60
They think not, then, which side the cause shall leese,
    Nor how to get the lawyer fees.
Such, and no other, was that age, of old,
    Which boasts to have had the head of gold.
And such since thou canst make thine own content,
    Strive, Wroth, to live long innocent.
Let others watch in guilty arms, and stand
    The fury of a rash command,
Go enter breaches, meet the cannons' rage,
    That they may sleep with scars in age.   70
And show their feathers shot, and colours torn,
    And brag, that they were therefore born.
Let this man sweat, and wrangle at the bar,
    For every price, in every jar,
And change possessions, oft'ner with his breath,
    Than either money, war, or death:
Let him, than hardest sires, more disinherit,
    And eachwhere boast it as his merit,
To blow up orphans, widows, and their states;
    And think his power doth equal Fate's.   80
Let that go heap a mass of wretched wealth,
    Purchased by rapine, worse than stealth,
And brooding o'er it sit, with broadest eyes,
    Not doing good, scarce when he dies.
Let thousands more go flatter vice, and win,
    By being organs to great sin,

Get place, and honour, and be glad to keep
　　The secrets, that shall break their sleep:
And, so they ride in purple, eat in plate,
90　　Though poison, think it a great fate.
But thou, my Wroth, if I can truth apply,
　　Shalt neither that, nor this envy:
Thy peace is made; and, when man's state is well,
　　'Tis better, if he there can dwell.
God wisheth, none should wrack on a strange shelf:
　　To him, man's dearer, than t'himself.
And, howsoever we may think things sweet,
　　He always gives what he knows meet;
Which who can use is happy: such be thou.
100　　Thy morning's, and thy evening's vow
Be thanks to him, and earnest prayer, to find
　　A body sound, with sounder mind;
To do thy country service, thyself right;
　　That neither want do thee affright,
Nor death; but when thy latest sand is spent,
　　Thou mayst think life, a thing but lent.

To the World

∽

(A FAREWELL FOR A GENTLEWOMAN,
VIRTUOUS AND NOBLE)
False world, goodnight: since thou hast brought
　　That hour upon my morn of age,
Henceforth I quit thee from my thought,
　　My part is ended on thy stage.
Do not once hope, that thou canst tempt
　　A spirit so resolved to tread
Upon thy throat, and live exempt
　　From all the nets that thou canst spread.

I know thy forms are studied arts,
 Thy subtle ways, be narrow straits; 10
Thy courtesy but sudden starts,
 And what thou call'st thy gifts are baits.
I know too, though thou strut, and paint,
 Yet art thou both shrunk up, and old,
That only fools make thee a saint,
 And all thy good is to be sold.
I know thou whole art but a shop
 Of toys, and trifles, traps, and snares,
To take the weak, or make them stop:
 Yet art thou falser than thy wares. 20
And, knowing this, should I yet stay,
 Like such as blow away their lives,
And never will redeem a day,
 Enamoured of their golden gyves?
Or, having 'scaped, shall I return,
 And thrust my neck into the noose,
From whence, so lately, I did burn,
 With all my powers, myself to loose?
What bird, or beast, is known so dull,
 That fled his cage, or broke his chain, 30
And tasting air, and freedom, wull
 Render his head in there again?
If these, who have but sense, can shun
 The engines, that have them annoyed;
Little, for me, had reason done,
 If I could not thy gins avoid.
Yes, threaten, do. Alas I fear
 As little, as I hope from thee:
I know thou canst nor show, nor bear
 More hatred, than thou hast to me. 40
My tender, first, and simple years
 Thou didst abuse, and then betray;
Since stirred'st up jealousies and fears,
 When all the causes were away.
Then, in a soil hast planted me,
 Where breathe the basest of thy fools;

Where envious arts professéd be,
    And pride, and ignorance the schools,
Where nothing is examined, weighed,
50   But, as 'tis rumoured, so believed:
Where every freedom is betrayed,
    And every goodness taxed, or grieved.
But, what we are born for, we must bear:
    Our frail condition it is such,
That, what to all may happen here,
    If't chance to me, I must not grutch.
Else, I my state should much mistake,
    To harbour a divided thought
From all my kind: that, for my sake,
60   There should a miracle be wrought.
No, I do know, that I was born
    To age, misfortune, sickness, grief:
But I will bear these, with that scorn,
    As shall not need thy false relief.
Nor for my peace will I go far,
    As wanderers do, that still do roam,
But make my strengths, such as they are,
    Here in my bosom, and at home.

Song. To Celia

Come my Celia, let us prove,
    While we may, the sports of love;
Time will not be ours, for ever:
    He, at length, our good will sever.
Spend not then his gifts in vain.
    Suns, that set, may rise again:

But if once we lose this light,
'Tis, with us, perpetual night.
Why should we defer our joys?
Fame, and rumour are but toys.   10
Cannot we delude the eyes
Of a few poor household spies?
Or his easier ears beguile,
So removèd by our wile?
'Tis no sin, love's fruit to steal,
But the sweet theft to reveal:
To be taken, to be seen,
These have crimes accounted been.

To the Same

∞

Kiss me, sweet: the wary lover
Can your favours keep, and cover,
When the common courting jay
All your bounties will betray.
Kiss again: no creature comes.
Kiss, and score up wealthy sums
On my lips, thus hardly sundered,
While you breathe. First give a hundred,
Then a thousand, then another
Hundred, then unto the tother   10
Add a thousand, and so more:
Till you equal with the store,
All the grass that Romney yields,
Or the sands in Chelsea fields,
Or the drops in silver Thames,
Or the stars, that gild his streams,

In the silent summer nights,
When youths ply their stol'n delights.
That the curious may not know
20 How to tell them as they flow,
And the envious, when they find,
What their number is, be pined.

Song. That Women Are But Men's Shadows

Follow a shadow, it still flies you;
Seem to fly it, it will pursue:
So court a mistress, she denies you;
Let her alone, she will court you.
Say, are not women truly, then,
Styled but the shadows of us men?
At morn, and even, shades are longest;
At noon, they are or short, or none:
So men at weakest, they are strongest,
10 But grant us perfect, they're not known.
Say, are not women truly, then,
Styled but the shadows of us men?

To Sickness

Why, disease, dost thou molest
Ladies, and of them the best?
Do not men, ynow of rites
To thy altars, by their nights

Spent in surfeits: and their days,
And nights too, in worser ways?
Take heed, sickness, what you do,
I shall fear, you'll surfeit too.
Live not we, as, all thy stalls,
Spittles, pest-house, hospitals,   10
Scarce will take our present store?
And this age will build no more:
Pray thee, feed contented, then,
Sickness, only on us men.
Or if needs thy lust will taste
Womankind; devour the waste
Livers, round about the town.
But, forgive me, with thy crown
They maintain the truest trade,
And have more diseases made.   20
What should, yet, thy palate please?
Daintiness, and softer ease,
Sleekéd limbs, and finest blood?
If thy leanness love such food,
There are those, that, for thy sake,
Do enough; and who would take
Any pains; yea, think it price,
To become thy sacrifice.
That distil their husbands' land
In decoctions; and are manned   30
With ten emp'rics, in their chamber,
Lying for the spirit of amber.
That for the oil of Talc, dare spend
More than citizens dare lend
Them, and all their officers.
That, to make all pleasure theirs,
Will by coach, and water go,
Every stew in town to know;
Dare entail their loves on any,
Bald, or blind, or ne'er so many: 40
And, for thee, at common game,
Play away, health, wealth, and fame.

63

These, disease, will thee deserve:
And will, long ere thou shouldst starve,
On their beds, most prostitute,
Move it, as their humblest suit,
In thy justice to molest
None but them, and leave the rest.

Song. To Celia

Drink to me, only, with thine eyes,
    And I will pledge with mine;
Or leave a kiss but in the cup,
    And I'll not look for wine.
The thirst, that from the soul doth rise,
    Doth ask a drink divine:
But might I of Jove's nectar sup,
    I would not change for thine.
I sent thee, late, a rosy wreath,
10   Not so much honouring thee,
As giving it a hope, that there
    It could not withered be.
But thou thereon didst only breathe,
    And sent'st it back to me:
Since when it grows, and smells, I swear,
    Not of itself, but thee.

'And must I sing? What subject shall I choose?'

∽

And must I sing? What subject shall I choose?
Or whose great name in poets' heaven use,
For the more countenance to my active muse?

Hercules? Alas his bones are yet sore,
With his old earthly labours. T'exact more,
Of his dull godhead, were sin. I'll implore

Phoebus. No? Tend thy cart still. Envious day
Shall not give out, that I have made thee stay,
And foundered thy hot team, to tune my lay.

Nor will I beg of thee, lord of the vine,   10
To raise my spirits with thy conjuring wine,
In the green circle of thy ivy twine.

Pallas, nor thee I call on, mankind maid,
That, at thy birth, mad'st the poor smith afraid,
Who, with his axe, thy father's midwife played.

Go, cramp dull Mars, light Venus, when he snorts,
Or, with thy tribade trine, invent new sports,
Thou, nor thy looseness, with my making sorts.

Let the old boy, your son, ply his old task,
Turn the stale prologue to some painted masque,   20
His absence in my verse, is all I ask.

Hermes, the cheater, shall not mix with us,
Though he would steal his sisters' Pegasus,
And riffle him: or pawn his Petasus.

Nor all the ladies of the Thespian lake,
(Though they were crushed into one form) could make
A beauty of that merit, that should take

My muse up by commission: no, I bring
My own true fire. Now my thought takes wing,
30   And now an epode to deep ears I sing.

Epode
∽

Not to know vice at all, and keep true state,
  Is virtue, and not Fate:
Next, to that virtue, is to know vice well,
  And her black spite expel.
Which to effect (since no breast is so sure,
  Or safe, but she'll procure
Some way of entrance) we must plant a guard
  Of thoughts to watch, and ward
At the eye and ear (the ports unto the mind)
10   That no strange, or unkind
Object arrive there, but the heart (our spy)
  Give knowledge instantly,
To wakeful reason, our affections' king:
  Who (in the examining)
Will quickly taste the treason, and commit
  Close, the close cause of it.
'Tis the securest policy we have,
  To make our sense our slave.
But this true course is not embraced by many:
20   By many? Scarce by any.
For either our affections do rebel,
  Or else the sentinel
(That should ring 'larum to the heart) doth sleep,
  Or some great thought doth keep
Back the intelligence, and falsely swears,
  They are base, and idle fears

Whereof the loyal conscience so complains.
   Thus, by these subtle trains,
Do several passions still invade the mind,
   And strike our reason blind.   30
Of which usurping rank, some have thought love
   The first; as prone to move
Most frequent tumults, horrors, and unrests,
   In our inflamèd breasts:
But this doth from the cloud of error grow,
   Which thus we overblow,
The thing, they here call love, is blind desire,
   Armed with bow, shafts, and fire;
Inconstant, like the sea, of whence 'tis born,
   Rough, swelling, like a storm: 40
With whom who sails, rides on the surge of fear,
   And boils, as if he were
In a continual tempest. Now, true love
   No such effects doth prove;
That is an essence far more gentle, fine,
   Pure, perfect, nay divine;
It is a golden chain let down from heaven,
   Whose links are bright, and even,
That falls like sleep on lovers, and combines
   The soft, and sweetest minds   50
In equal knots: this bears no brands, nor darts,
   To murther different hearts,
But, in a calm, and god-like unity,
   Preserves community.
O, who is he, that (in this peace) enjoys
   The elixir of all joys?
A form more fresh, than are the Eden bowers,
   And lasting, as her flowers:
Richer than time, and as time's virtue, rare:
   Sober, as saddest care: 60
A fixéd thought, an eye untaught to glance;
   Who (blessed with such high chance)
Would, at suggestion of a steep desire,
   Cast himself from the spire

Of all his happiness? But soft: I hear
    Some vicious fool draw near,
That cries, we dream, and swears, there's no such thing,
    As this chaste love we sing.
Peace, luxury, thou art like one of those
70   Who, being at sea, suppose,
Because they move, the continent doth so:
    No, vice, we let thee know
Though thy wild thoughts with sparrows' wings do fly
    Turtles can chastely die;
And yet (in this to express ourselves more clear)
    We do not number, here,
Such spirits as are only continent,
    Because lust's means are spent:
Or those, who doubt the common mouth of fame,
80   And for their place, and name,
Cannot so safely sin. Their chastity
    Is mere necessity.
Nor mean we those, whom vows and conscience
    Have filled with abstinence:
Though we acknowledge, who can so abstain,
    Makes a most blessèd gain.
He that for love of goodness hateth ill,
    Is more crown-worthy still,
Than he, which for sin's penalty forbears.
90   His heart sins, though he fears.
But we propose a person like our dove,
    Graced with a phoenix love;
A beauty of that clear, and sparkling light,
    Would make a day of night,
And turn the blackest sorrows to bright joys:
    Whose odorous breath destroys
All taste of bitterness, and makes the air
    As sweet, as she is fair.
A body so harmoniously composed,
100   As if nature disclosed
All her best symmetry in that one feature!
    O, so divine a creature

Who could be false to? Chiefly, when he knows
    How only she bestows
The wealthy treasure of her love on him;
    Making his fortunes swim
In the full flood of her admired perfection?
    What savage, brute affection,
Would not be fearful to offend a dame
    Of this excelling frame?   110
Much more a noble, and right generous mind
    (To virtuous moods inclined)
That knows the weight of guilt: he will refrain
    From thoughts of such a strain.
And to his sense object this sentence ever,
    Man may securely sin, but safely never.

Epistle to Elizabeth, Countess of Rutland

∽

Madam,
Whilst that, for which, all virtue now is sold,
And almost every vice, almighty gold,
That which, to boot with hell, is thought worth heaven,
And, for it, life, conscience, yea, souls are given,
Toils, by grave custom, up and down the court,
To every squire, or groom, that will report
Well, or ill, only, all the following year,
Just to the weight their this day's presents bear;
While it makes huishers serviceable men,
And some one apteth to be trusted, then,   10
Though never after; whiles it gains the voice
Of some grand peer, whose air doth make rejoice
The fool that gave it; who will want, and weep,
When his proud patron's favours are asleep;

While thus it buys great grace, and hunts poor fame;
Runs between man, and man; 'tween dame, and dame;
Solders cracked friendship; makes love last a day;
Or perhaps less: whilst gold bears all this sway,
I, that have none (to send you) send you verse.
20 A present, which (if elder writs rehearse
The truth of times) was once of more esteem,
Than this, our gilt, nor golden age can deem,
When gold was made no weapon to cut throats,
Or put to flight Astrea, when her ingots
Were yet unfound, and better placed in earth,
Than, here, to give pride fame, and peasants birth.
But let this dross carry what price it will
With noble ignorants, and let them still,
Turn, upon scorned verse, their quarter-face:
30 With you, I know, my offering will find grace.
For what a sin 'gainst your great father's spirit,
Were it to think, that you should not inherit
His love unto the muses, when his skill
Almost you have, or may have, when you will?
Wherein wise Nature you a dowry gave,
Worth an estate, treble to that you have.
Beauty, I know, is good, and blood is more;
Riches thought most: but, madam, think what store
The world hath seen, which all these had in trust,
40 And now lie lost in their forgotten dust.
It is the muse, alone, can raise to heaven,
And, at her strong arms' end, hold up, and even,
The souls, she loves. Those other glorious notes,
Inscribed in touch or marble, or the coats
Painted, or carved upon our great men's tombs,
Or in their windows; do but prove the wombs,
That bred them, graves: when they were born, they died,
That had no muse to make their fame abide.
How many equal with the Argive queen,
50 Have beauty known, yet none so famous seen?
Achilles was not first, that valiant was,
Or, in an army's head, that, locked in brass,

Gave killing strokes. There were brave men, before
Ajax, or Idomen, or all the store,
That Homer brought to Troy; yet none so live:
Because they lacked the sacred pen, could give
Like life unto them. Who heaved Hercules
Unto the stars? Or the Tyndarides?
Who placèd Jason's Argo in the sky?
Or set bright Ariadne's crown so high?   60
Who made a lamp of Berenice's hair?
Or lifted Cassiopea in her chair?
But only poets, rapt with rage divine?
And such, or my hopes fail, shall make you shine.
You, and that other star, that purest light,
Of all Lucina's train; Lucy the bright.
Than which a nobler heaven itself knows not.
Who, though she have a better verser got,
(Or poet, in the court account) than I,
And, who doth me (though I not him) envy,   70
Yet, for the timely favours she hath done,
To my less sanguine muse, wherein she hath won
My grateful soul, the subject of her powers,
I have already used some happy hours,
To her remembrance; which when time shall bring
To curious light, the notes I then shall sing,
Will prove old Orpheus' act no tale to be:
For I shall move stocks, stones, no less than he.
Then all, that have but done my muse least grace,
Shall thronging come, and boast the happy place   80
They hold in my strange poems, which, as yet,
Had not their form touched by an English wit.
There like a rich, and golden pyramid,
Borne up by statues, shall I rear your head,
Above your under-carvéd ornaments,
And show, how, to the life, my soul presents
Your form ímpressed there: not with tickling rhymes,
Or commonplaces, filched, that take these times,
But high, and noble matter, such as flies
From brains entranced, and filled with ecstasies;   90

71

Moods, which the godlike Sidney oft did prove,
And your brave friend, and mine so well did love.
Who wheresoe'er he be, on what dear coast,
Now thinking on you, though to England lost,
For that firm grace he holds in your regard,
I, that am grateful for him, have prepared
This hasty sacrifice, wherein I rear
A vow as new, and ominous as the year,
Before his swift and circled race be run,
100   My best of wishes, may you bear a son.

Epistle. To Katherine, Lady Aubigny

'Tis grown almost a danger to speak true
Of any good mind, now: there are so few.
The bad, by number, are so fortified,
As what they have lost to expect, they dare deride.
So both the praised, and praisers suffer: yet,
For others' ill, ought none their good forget.
I, therefore, who profess myself in love
With every virtue, wheresoe'er it move,
And howsoever; as I am at feud
10   With sin and vice, though with a throne endued;
And, in this name, am given out dangerous
By arts, and practice of the vicious,
Such as suspect themselves, and think it fit
For their own cap'tal crimes, t'indict my wit;
I, that have suffered this; and, though forsook
Of Fortune, have not altered yet my look,
Or so myself abandoned, as because
Men are not just, or keep no holy laws
Of nature, and society, I should faint;
20   Or fear to draw true lines, 'cause others paint:

I, madam, am become your praiser. Where,
If it may stand with your soft blush to hear
Yourself but told unto yourself, and see
In my chárácter, what your features be,
You will not from the paper slightly pass:
No lady, but, at some time, loves her glass.
And this shall be no false one, but as much
Removed, as you from need to have it such.
Look then, and see yourself. I will not say
Your beauty; for you see that every day:　　　　30
And so do many more. All which can call
It perfect, proper, pure, and natural,
Not taken up o' the doctors, but as well
As I, can say, and see it doth excel.
That asks but to be censured by the eyes;
And, in those outward forms, all fools are wise.
Nor that your beauty wanted not a dower,
Do I reflect. Some alderman has power,
Or cozening farmer of the customs so,
To advance his doubtful issue, and o'erflow　　　　40
A prince's fortune: these are gifts of chance,
And raise not virtue; they may vice enhance.
My mirror is more subtle, clear, refined,
And takes, and gives the beauties of the mind.
Though it reject not those of Fortune: such
As blood, and match. Wherein, how more than much
Are you engagèd to your happy fate,
For such a lot! That mixed you with a state
Of so great title, birth, but virtue most,
Without which, all the rest were sounds, or lost.　　　　50
'Tis only that can time, and chance defeat:
For he, that once is good, is ever great.
Wherewith, then, madam, can you better pay
This blessing of your stars, than by that way
Of virtue, which you tread? What if alone?
Without companions? 'Tis safe to have none.
In single paths, dangers with ease are watched:
Contagion in the press is soonest catched.

This makes, that wisely you decline your life,
60 Far from the maze of custom, error, strife,
And keep an even, and unaltered gait;
Not looking by, or back (like those, that wait
Times, and occasions, to start forth, and seem)
Which though the turning world may disesteem,
Because that studies spectacles, and shows,
And after varied, as fresh objects goes,
Giddy with change, and therefore cannot see
Right, the right way: yet must your comfort be
Your conscience, and not wonder, if none asks
70 For truth's complexion, where they all wear masks.
Let who will follow fashions, and attires,
Maintain their liegers forth, for foreign wires,
Melt down their husbands' land, to pour away
On the close groom, and page, on New Year's Day,
And almost all days after, while they live;
(They find it both so witty, and safe to give).
Let them on powders, oils, and paintings, spend,
Till that no usurer, nor his bawds dare lend
Them, or their officers: and no man know,
80 Whether it be a face they wear, or no.
Let them waste body, and state; and after all,
When their own parasites laugh at their fall,
May they have nothing left, whereof they can
Boast, but how oft they have gone wrong to man:
And call it their brave sin. For such there be
That do sin only for the infamy:
And never think, how vice doth every hour,
Eat on her clients, and some one devour.
You, madam, young have learned to shun these shelves,
90 Whereon the most of mankind wrack themselves,
And, keeping a just course, have early put
Into your harbour, and all passage shut
'Gainst storms, or pirates, that might charge your peace;
For which you worthy are the glad increase
Of your blessed womb, made fruitful from above,
To pay your lord the pledges of chaste love:

And raise a noble stem, to give the fame
To Clifton's blood, that is denied their name.
Grow, grow, fair tree, and as thy branches shoot,
Hear, what the muses sing about thy root,   100
By me, their priest (if they can aught divine)
Before the moons have filled their triple trine,
To crown the burthen which you go withall,
It shall a ripe and timely issue fall,
To expect the honours of great Aubigny:
And greater rites, yet writ in mystery,
But which the Fates forbid me to reveal.
Only, thus much, out of a ravished zeal,
Unto your name, and goodness of your life,
They speak; since you are truly that rare wife,   110
Other great wives may blush at: when they see
What your tried manners are, what theirs should be.
How you love one, and him you should; how still
You are depending on his word, and will;
Not fashioned for the court, or strangers' eyes;
But to please him, who is the dearer prize
Unto himself, by being so dear to you.
This makes, that your affections still be new,
And that your souls conspire, as they were gone
Each into other, and had now made one.   120
Live that one, still; and as long years do pass,
Madam, be bold to use this truest glass:
Wherein, your form, you still the same shall find;
Because nor it can change, nor such a mind.

Ode. To Sir William Sidney,
on His Birthday

∞

Now that the hearth is crowned with smiling fire,
　And some do drink, and some do dance,
　　　Some ring,
　　　Some sing,
　And all do strive to advance
The gladness higher:
　　　Wherefore should I
　　　Stand silent by,
　　　　Who not the least,
10　　　Both love the cause, and authors of the feast?

Give me my cup, but from the Thespian well,
　That I may tell to Sidney, what
　　　This day
　　　Doth say,
　And he may think on that
Which I do tell:
　　　When all the noise
　　　Of these forced joys,
　　　　Are fled and gone,
20　　　And he, with his best genius left alone.

This day says, then, the number of glad years
　Are justly summed, that make you man;
　　　Your vow
　　　Must now
　Strive all right ways it can,
To outstrip your peers:
　　　Since he doth lack
　　　Of going back
　　　　Little, whose will
30　　　Doth urge him to run wrong, or to stand still.

Nor can a little of the common store,
  Of nobles' virtue, show in you;
      Your blood
      So good
And great, must seek for new,
And study more:
    Not weary, rest
    On what's deceased.
      For they, that swell
      With dust of ancestors, in graves but dwell.   40

'Twas be exacted of your name, whose son,
  Whose nephew, whose grand-child you are;
      And men
      Will, then,
Say you have followed far,
When well begun:
    Which must be now,
    They teach you, how.
      And he that stays
      To live until tomorrow hath lost two days.   50

So may you live in honour, as in name,
  If with this truth you be inspired,
      So may
      This day
Be more, and long desired:
And with the flame,
    Of love be bright,
    As with the light
      Of bone-fires. Then
      The birthday shines, when logs not burn, but   60
men.

To Heaven

∞

Good, and great God, can I not think of thee,
But it must, straight, my melancholy be?
Is it interpreted in me disease,
That, laden with my sins, I seek for ease?
O, be thou witness, that the reins dost know,
And hearts of all, if I be sad for show,
And judge me after: if I dare pretend
To aught but grace, or aim at other end.
As thou art all, so be thou all to me,
First, midst, and last, converted one, and three;
My faith, my hope, my love: and in this state,
My judge, my witness, and my advocate.
Where have I been this while exiled from thee?
And whither rapt, now thou but stoop'st to me?
Dwell, dwell here still: O, being everywhere,
How can I doubt to find thee ever, here?
I know my state, both full of shame, and scorn,
Conceived in sin, and unto labour born,
Standing with fear, and must with horror fall,
And destined unto judgment, after all.
I feel my griefs too, and there scarce is ground,
Upon my flesh to inflict another wound.
Yet dare I not complain, or wish for death
With holy Paul, lest it be thought the breath
Of discontent; or that these prayers be
For weariness of life, not love of thee.

UNDERWOODS

Poems of Devotion

THE SINNER'S SACRIFICE

(TO THE HOLY TRINITY)
1. O holy, blessèd, glorious Trinity
   Of persons, still one God, in unity,
   The faithful man's believèd mystery,
       Help, help to lift

2. Myself up to thee, harrowed, torn, and bruised
   By sin, and Satan; and my flesh misused,
   As my heart lies in pieces, all confused,
       O take my gift.

3. All-gracious God, the sinner's sacrifice,
   A broken heart thou wert not wont despise,   10
   But 'bove the fat of rams, or bulls, to prize
       An offering meet,

4. For thy acceptance. O, behold me right,
   And take compassion on my grievous plight.
   What odour can be, than a heart contrite,
       To thee more sweet?

5. Eternal Father, God, who didst create
   This all of nothing, gav'st it form, and fate,
   And breath'st into it, life, and light, with state
       To worship thee.   20

79

6. Eternal God the Son, who not denied'st
   To take our nature; becam'st man, and died'st,
   To pay our debts, upon thy cross, and cried'st
       All's done in me.

7. Eternal Spirit, God from both proceeding,
   Father and Son; the comforter, in breeding
   Pure thoughts in man: with fiery zeal them feeding
       For acts of grace.

8. Increase those acts, O glorious Trinity
   Of persons, still one God in unity;
   Till I attain the longed-for mystery
       Of seeing your face.

9. Beholding one in three, and three in one,
   A Trinity, to shine in union;
   The gladdest light, dark man can think upon;
       O grant it me!

10. Father, and Son, and Holy Ghost, you three
    All coëternal in your majesty,
    Distinct in persons, yet in unity
        One God to see.

11. My maker, saviour, and my sanctifier,
    To hear, to mediate, sweeten my desire,
    With grace, with love, with cherishing entire,
        O, then how blessed;

12. Among thy saints elected to abide,
    And with thy angels, placèd side by side,
    But in thy presence truly glorified
        Shall I there rest!

A HYMN TO GOD THE FATHER

Hear me, O God!
  A broken heart,
   Is my best part:
Use still thy rod,
  That I may prove
   Therein, thy love.

If thou hadst not
  Been stern to me,
   But left me free,
I had forgot   10
  Myself and thee.

For, sin's so sweet,
  As minds ill bent
   Rarely repent,
Until they meet
  Their punishment.

Who more can crave
  Than thou hast done:
   That gav'st a Son,
To free a slave?   20
  First made of nought;
   With all since bought.

Sin, death, and hell,
  His glorious name
   Quite overcame,
Yet I rebel,
  And slight the same.

But, I'll come in,
  Before my loss
   Me farther toss,   30
As sure to win
  Under his cross.

A HYMN ON THE NATIVITY OF MY SAVIOUR

I sing the birth, was born tonight,
The author both of life, and light;
   The angels so did sound it,
And like the ravished shepherds said,
Who saw the light, and were afraid,
   Yet searched, and true they found it.

The son of God, the eternal king,
That did us all salvation bring,
   And freed the soul from danger;
10 He whom the whole world could not take,
The Word, which heaven, and earth did make;
   Was now laid in a manger.

The Father's wisdom willed it so,
The Son's obedience knew no no,
   Both wills were in one stature;
And as that wisdom had decreed,
The word was now made flesh indeed,
   And took on him our nature.

What comfort by him do we win,
20 Who made himself the price of sin,
   To make us heirs of glory?
To see this babe, all innocence;
A martyr born in our defence;
   Can man forget this story?

A Celebration of Charis in Ten Lyric Pieces

∞

1 HIS EXCUSE FOR LOVING

Let it not your wonder move,
Less your laughter; that I love.
Though I now write fifty years,
I have had, and have my peers;
Poets, though divine, are men:
Some have loved as old again.
And it is not always face,
Clothes, or fortune gives the grace;
Or the feature, or the youth:
But the language, and the truth,   10
With the ardour, and the passion,
Gives the lover weight and fashion.
If you then will read the story,
First prepare you to be sorry,
That you never knew till now,
Either whom to love, or how:
But be glad, as soon with me,
When you know, that this is she,
Of whose beauty it was sung,
She shall make the old man young,   20
Keep the middle age at stay,
And let nothing high decay,
Till she be the reason why,
All the world for love may die.

2 HOW HE SAW HER

I beheld her, on a day,
When her look outflourished May:
And her dressing did out-brave

All the pride the fields then have:
Far I was from being stupid,
For I ran and called on Cupid:
Love if thou wilt ever see
Mark of glory, come with me;
Where's thy quiver? Bend thy bow:
10   Here's a shaft, thou art too slow!
And (withal) I did untie
Every cloud about his eye;
But, he had not gained his sight
Sooner, than he lost his might,
Or his courage; for away
Straight he ran, and durst not stay,
Letting bow and arrow fall,
Nor for any threat, or call,
Could be brought once back to look.
20   I fool-hardy, there uptook
Both the arrow he had quit,
And the bow: with thought to hit
This my object. But she threw
Such a lightning (as I drew)
At my face, that took my sight,
And my motion from me quite;
So that there, I stood a stone,
Mocked of all: and called of one
(Which with grief and wrath I heard)
30   Cupid's statue with a beard,
Or else one that played his ape,
In a Hercules his shape.

3 WHAT HE SUFFERED

After many scorns like these,
Which the prouder beauties please,
She content was to restore
Eyes and limbs, to hurt me more,

And would on conditions, be
Reconciled to love, and me:
First, that I must kneeling yield
Both the bow, and shaft I held
Unto her; which Love might take
At her hand, with oath, to make   10
Me, the scope of his next draught
Aimèd, with that self-same shaft.
He no sooner heard the law,
But the arrow home did draw
And (to gain her by his art)
Left it sticking in my heart:
Which when she beheld to bleed,
She repented of the deed,
And would fain have changed the fate,
But the pity comes too late.   20
Loser-like, now, all my wreak
Is, that I have leave to speak,
And in either prose, or song,
To revenge me with my tongue,
Which how dexterously I do
Hear and make example too.

4 HER TRIUMPH

See the chariot at hand here of Love
    Wherein my lady rideth!
Each that draws, is a swan, or a dove,
    And well the car Love guideth.
As she goes, all hearts do duty
        Unto her beauty;
And enamoured, do wish, so they might
        But enjoy such a sight,
That they still were, to run by her side,
Through swords, through seas, whither she would ride.   10

Do but look on her eyes, they do light
  All that Love's world compriseth!
Do but look on her hair, it is bright
  As Love's star when it riseth!
Do but mark her forehead's smoother
    Than words that sooth her!
And from her archèd brows, such a grace
    Sheds itself through the face,
As alone there triumphs to the life
20 All the gain, all the good, of the elements' strife.

Have you seen but a bright lily grow,
  Before rude hands have touched it?
Ha' you marked but the fall o' the snow
  Before the soil hath smutched it?
Ha' you felt the wool o' the beaver,
    Or swansdown ever?
Or have smelt o' the bud o' the briar,
    Or the nard in the fire?
Or have tasted the bag of the bee?
30 O so white! O so soft! O so sweet is she!

5 HIS DISCOURSE WITH CUPID

Noblest Charis, you that are
Both my fortune, and my star!
And do govern more my blood,
Than the various moon the flood!
Hear, what late discourse of you,
Love, and I have had; and true.
'Mongst my muses finding me,
Where he chanced your name to see
Set, and to this softer strain;
10 Sure, said he, if I have brain,
This here sung, can be no other
By description, but my mother!
So hath Homer praised her hair;

So, Anacreon drawn the air
Of her face, and made to rise
Just about her sparkling eyes,
Both her brows, bent like my bow.
By her looks I do her know,
Which you call my shafts. And see!
Such my mother's blushes be,   20
As the bath your verse discloses
In her cheeks, of milk, and roses;
Such as oft I wanton in!
And, above her even chin,
Have you placed the bank of kisses,
Where, you say, men gather blisses,
Ripened with a breath more sweet,
Than when flowers, and west winds meet.
Nay, her white and polished neck,
With the lace that doth it deck,   30
Is my mother's! Hearts of slain
Lovers, made into a chain!
And between each rising breast,
Lies the valley, called my nest,
Where I sit and proin my wings
After flight; and put new strings
To my shafts! Her very name,
With my mother's is the same.
I confess all, I replied,
And the glass hangs by her side,   40
And the girdle 'bout her waist,
All is Venus: save unchaste.
But alas, thou see'st the least
Of her good, who is the best
Of her sex; but couldst thou, Love,
Call to mind the forms, that strove
For the apple, and those three
Make in one, the same were she.
For this beauty yet doth hide,
Something more than thou hast spied.   50
Outward grace weak love beguiles:

She is Venus, when she smiles,
But she's Juno, when she walks,
And Minerva, when she talks.

6 CLAIMING A SECOND KISS BY DESERT

Charis, guess, and do not miss,
Since I drew a morning kiss
From your lips, and sucked an air
Thence, as sweet, as you are fair,
What my muse and I have done:
Whether we have lost, or won,
If by us, the odds were laid,
That the bride (allowed a maid)
Looked not half so fresh, and fair,
10 With the advantage of her hair,
And her jewels, to the view
Of the assembly, as did you!
Or, that did you sit, or walk,
You were more the eye, and talk
Of the court, today, than all
Else that glistered in Whitehall;
So, as those that had your sight,
Wished the bride were changed tonight,
And did think, such rites were due
20 To no other grace but you!
Or, if you did move tonight
In the dances, with what spite
Of your peers, you were beheld,
That at every motion swelled
So to see a lady tread,
As might all the Graces lead,
And was worthy (being so seen)
To be envied of the queen.
Or if you would yet have stayed,

88

Whether any would upbraid   30
To himself his loss of time;
Or have charged his sight of crime,
To have left all sight for you:
Guess of these, which is the true;
And, if such a verse as this,
May not claim another kiss.

7 BEGGING ANOTHER, ON COLOUR OF
MENDING THE FORMER

For Love's sake, kiss me once again,
    I long, and should not beg in vain,
      Here's none to spy, or see;
        Why do you doubt, or stay?
   I'll taste as lightly as the bee,
That doth but touch his flower, and flies away.
    Once more, and (faith) I will be gone.
    Can he that loves, ask less than one?
      Nay, you may err in this,
        And all your bounty wrong: 10
   This could be called but half a kiss.
What w'are but once to do, we should do long.
    I will but mend the last, and tell
    Where, how it would have relished well;
      Join lip to lip, and try:
        Each sucks out other's breath.
    And whilst our tongues perplexèd lie,
Let who will think us dead, or wish our death.

8 URGING HER OF A PROMISE

Charis one day in discourse
Had of Love, and of his force,
Lightly promised, she would tell
What a man she could love well:
And that promise set on fire
All that heard her, with desire.
With the rest, I long expected,
When the work would be effected:
But we find that cold delay,
10   And excuse spun every day,
As, until she tell her one,
We all fear, she loveth none.
Therefore, Charis, you must do't,
For I will so urge you to't
You shall neither eat, nor sleep,
No, nor forth your window peep,
With your emissary eye,
To fetch in the forms go by:
And pronounce, which band or lace,
20   Better fits him, than his face;
Nay I will not let you sit
'Fore your idol glass a whit,
To say over every purl
There; or to reform a curl;
Or with secretary Sis
To consult, if fucus this
Be as good, as was the last:
All your sweet of life is past,
Make account unless you can,
30   (And that quickly) speak your man.

9 HER MAN DESCRIBED BY HER OWN DICTAMEN

Of your trouble, Ben, to ease me,
I will tell what man would please me.
I would have him if I could,
Noble; or of greater blood:
Titles, I confess, do take me;
And a woman God did make me.
French to boot, at least in fashion,
And his manners of that nation.
Young I'd have him too, and fair,
Yet a man; with crispèd hair   10
Cast in thousand snares, and rings
For Love's fingers, and his wings:
Chestnut colour, or more slack
Gold, upon a ground of black.
Venus', and Minerva's eyes
For he must look wanton-wise.
Eye-brows bent like Cupid's bow,
Front, an ample field of snow;
Even nose, and cheek (withal)
Smooth as is the billiard ball: 20
Chin, as woolly as the peach;
And his lip should kissing teach,
Till he cherished too much beard,
And make Love or me afeared.
He would have a hand as soft
As the down, and show it oft;
Skin as smooth as any rush,
And so thin to see a blush
Rising through it ere it came;
All his blood should be a flame   30
Quickly fired as in beginners
In love's school, and yet no sinners.
'Twere too long to speak of all:
What we harmony do call
In a body should be there.
Well he should his clothes to wear;

Yet no tailor help to make him;
Dressed, you still for man should take him;
And not think he'd eat a stake,
40   Or were set up in a brake.
Valiant he should be as fire,
Showing danger more than ire;
Bounteous as the clouds to earth;
And as honest as his birth.
All his action to be such,
As to do no thing too much.
Nor o'er-praise, nor yet condemn;
Nor out-value, nor contemn:
Nor do wrongs, nor wrongs receive;
50   Nor tie knots, nor knots unweave;
And from baseness to be free,
As he durst love truth and me.
Such a man, with every part,
I could give my very heart;
But of one, if short he came,
I can rest me where I am.

10 ANOTHER LADY'S EXCEPTION,
PRESENT AT THE HEARING

For his mind, I do not care,
That's a toy, that I could spare:
Let his title be but great,
His clothes rich, and band sit neat,
Himself young, and face be good,
All I wish is understood.
What you please, you parts may call,
'Tis one good part I'd lie withal.

The Hour-Glass

∞

Do but consider this small dust,
  Here running in the glass,
    By atoms moved;
Could you believe, that this,
  The body was
    — Of one that loved?
And in his mistress' flame, playing like a fly,
  Turned to cinders by her eye?
  Yes; and in death as life unblessed,
    To have't expressed,   10
Even ashes of lovers find no rest.

My Picture Left in Scotland

∞

I now think, Love is rather deaf, than blind,
  For else it could not be,
    That she,
Whom I adore so much, should so slight me,
  And cast my love behind:
I'm sure my language to her, was as sweet,
    And every close did meet
    In sentence, of as subtle feet,
      As hath the youngest he,
  That sits in shadow of Apollo's tree.   10
Oh, but my conscious fears,
    That fly my thoughts between,
    Tell me that she hath seen

My hundreds of grey hairs,
Told seven and forty years,
Read so much waist, as she cannot embrace
My mountain belly, and my rocky face,
And all these through her eyes, have stopped her ears.

Against Jealousy

∞

Wretched and foolish jealousy,
How cam'st thou thus to enter me?
    I ne'er was of thy kind;
   Nor have I yet the narrow mind
    To vent that poor desire,
That others should not warm them at my fire:
    I wish the sun should shine
On all men's fruit, and flowers, as well as mine.

But under the disguise of love
10 Thou say'st, thou only cam'st to prove
    What my affections were.
   Think'st thou that love is helped by fear?
    Go, get thee quickly forth;
Love's sickness, and his noted want of worth,
    Seek doubting men to please;
I ne'er will owe my health to a disease.

The Dream

∞

Or scorn, or pity on me take,
I must the true relation make,
   I am undone tonight;
   Love in a subtle dream disguised,
   Hath both my heart and me surprised,
Whom never yet he durst attempt awake;
Nor will he tell me for whose sake
     He did me the delight,
        Or spite,
   But leaves me to inquire,   10
   In all my wild desire
     Of sleep again; who was his aid;
     And sleep so guilty and afraid,
As since he dares not come within my sight.

An Epistle to Sir Edward Sackville, now Earl of Dorset

∞

If Sackville, all that have the power to do
Great and good turns, as well could time them too,
And knew their how, and where: we should have, then
Less list of proud, hard, or ingrateful men.
For benefits are owed with the same mind
As they are done, and such returns they find:
You then whose will not only, but desire
To succour my necessities took fire,
Not at my prayers, but your sense; which laid
The way to meet, what others would upbraid;   10

And in the act did so my blush prevent,
As I did feel it done, as soon as meant:
You cannot doubt, but I who freely know
This good from you, as freely will it owe;
And though my fortune humble me, to take
The smallest courtesies with thanks, I make
Yet choice from whom I take them; and would shame
To have such do me good, I durst not name:
They are the noblest benefits, and sink
20 Deepest in man, of which when he doth think,
The memory delights him more, from whom
Than what he hath received. Gifts stink from some,
They are so long a coming, and so hard;
Where any deed is forced, the grace is marred.

    Can I owe thanks, for courtesies received
Against his will that does them? That hath weaved
Excuses, or delays? Or done them scant,
That they have more oppressed me, than my want?
Or if he did it not to succour me,
30 But by mere chance? For interest? Or to free
Himself of further trouble, or the weight
Of pressure, like one taken in a strait?
All this corrupts the thanks; less hath he won,
That puts it in his debt-book ere it be done;
Or that doth sound a trumpet, and doth call
His grooms to witness; or else lets it fall
In that proud manner: as a good so gained
Must make me sad for what I have obtained.

    No! Gifts and thanks should have one cheerful face,
40 So each, that's done, and ta'en, becomes a brace.
He neither gives, or does, that doth delay
A benefit: or that doth throw't away,
No more than he doth thank, that will receive
Naught but in corners; and is loth to leave
Least air, or print, but flies it: such men would
Run from the conscience of it if they could.

    As I have seen some infants of the sword
Well known, and practised borrowers on their word,

Give thanks by stealth, and whispering in the ear,
For what they straight would to the world forswear; 50
And speaking worst of those, from whom they went
But then, fist filled, to put me off the scent.
Now damn me, sir, if you shall not command
My sword ('tis but a poor sword understand)
As far as any poor sword in the land;
Then turning unto him is next at hand,
Damns whom he damned too, is the veriest gull,
Has feathers, and will serve a man to pull.
 Are they not worthy to be answered so,
That to such natures let their full hands flow, 60
And seek not wants to succour: but inquire
Like money-brokers, after names, and hire
Their bounties forth, to him that last was made,
Or stands to be in commission of the blade?
Still, still, the hunters of false fame apply
Their thoughts and means to making loud the cry;
But one is bitten by the dog he fed,
And hurt seeks cure; the surgeon bids take bread,
And sponge-like with it dry up the blood quite:
Then give it to the hound that did him bite; 70
Pardon, says he, that were a way to see
All the town curs take each their snatch at me.
O, is it so? Knows he so much? And will
Feed those, at whom the table points at still?
I not deny it, but to help the need
Of any, is a great and generous deed:
Yea, of the ingrateful; and he forth must tell
Many a pound, and piece will place one well;
But these men ever want: their very trade
Is borrowing; that but stopped they do invade 80
All as their prize, turn pirates here at land,
Have their Bermudas, and their straits in the Strand:
Man out their boats to the Temple, and not shift
Now, but command; make tribute, what was gift;
And it is paid them with a trembling zeal,
And superstition I dare scarce reveal

If it were clear, but being so in cloud
Carried and wrapped, I only am allowed
My wonder why the taking a clown's purse,
90   Or robbing the poor market folks should nurse
Such a religious horror in the breasts
Of our town gallantry! Or why there rests
Such worship due to kicking of a punk!
Or swaggering with the watch, or drawer drunk;
Or feats of darkness acted in mid-sun,
And told of with more licence than they were done!
Sure there is mystery in it, I not know,
That men such reverence to such actions show!
And almost deify the authors! Make
100   Loud sacrifice of drink, for their health' sake
Rear-suppers in their names! And spend whole nights
Unto their praise, in certain swearing rites;
Cannot a man be reckoned in the state
Of valour, but at this idolatrous rate?
I thought that fortitude had been a mean
'Twixt fear and rashness: not a lust obscene,
Or appetite of offending, but a skill,
Or science of discerning good and ill.
And you, sir, know it well to whom I write,
110   That with these mixtures we put out her light.
Her ends are honesty, and public good!
And where they want, she is not understood.
No more are these of us, let them then go,
I have the list of mine own faults to know,
Look to and cure; he's not a man hath none,
But like to be, that every day mends one,
And feels it; else he tarries by the beast.
Can I discern how shadows are decreased,
Or grown, by height or lowness of the sun?
120   And can I less of substance? When I run,
Ride, sail, am coached, know I how far I have gone,
And my mind's motion not? Or have I none?
No! he must feel and know, that will advance.
Men have been great, but never good by chance,

Or on the sudden. It were strange that he
Who was this morning such a one, should be
Sidney ere night! Or that did go to bed
Coriat, should rise the most sufficient head
Of Christendom! And neither of these know
Were the rack offered them how they came so;   130
'Tis by degrees that men arrive at glad
Profit in aught; each day some little add,
In time 'twill be a heap; this is not true
Alone in money, but in manners too.
Yet we must more than move still, or go on,
We must accomplish; 'tis the last key-stone
That makes the arch. The rest that there were put
Are nothing till that comes to bind and shut.
Then stands it a triumphal mark! Then men
Observe the strength, the height, the why, and when,   140
It was erected; and still walking under
Meet some new matter to look up and wonder!
Such notes are virtuous men! They live as fast
As they are high; are rooted and will last.
They need no stilts, nor rise upon their toes,
As if they would belie their stature; those
Are dwarfs of honour, and have neither weight
Nor fashion; if they chance aspire to height,
'Tis like light canes, that first rise big and brave,
Shoot forth in smooth and comely spaces; have   150
But few and fair divisions: but being got
Aloft, grow less and straitened; full of knot;
And last, go out in nothing: you that see
Their difference, cannot choose which you will be.
You know (without my flattering you) too much
For me to be your indice. Keep you such,
That I may love your person (as I do)
Without your gift, though I can rate that too,
By thanking thus the courtesy to life,
Which you will bury, but therein, the strife   160
May grow so great to be example, when
(As their true rule or lesson) either men

Donors or donees to their practice shall
Find you to reckon nothing, me owe all.

An Epistle to Master John Selden

∞

I know to whom I write. Here, I am sure,
Though I am short, I cannot be obscure:
Less shall I for the art or dressing care;
Truth, and the Graces, best when naked are.
Your book, my Selden, I have read, and much
Was trusted, that you thought my judgement such
To ask it: though in most of works it be
A penance, where a man may not be free,
Rather than office, when it doth or may
10 Chance that the friend's affection proves allay
Unto the censure. Yours all need doth fly
Of this so vicious humanity,
Than which there is not unto study, a more
Pernicious enemy; we see before
A many of books, even good judgements wound
Themselves through favouring what is there not found:
But I on yours far otherwise shall do,
Not fly the crime, but the suspicion too:
Though I confess (as every muse hath erred,
20 And mine not least) I have too oft preferred
Men past their terms, and praised some names too much,
But 'twas with purpose to have made them such.
Since being deceived, I turn a sharper eye
Upon myself, and ask to whom, and why,
And what I write? And vex it many days
Before men get a verse: much less a praise;
So that my reader is assured, I now
Mean what I speak: and still will keep that vow.

Stand forth my object, then, you that have been
Ever at home: yet, have all countries seen: 30
And like a compass keeping one foot still
Upon your centre, do your circle fill
Of general knowledge; watched men, manners too,
Heard what times past have said, seen what ours do:
Which grace shall I make love to first? Your skill,
Or faith in things? Or is't your wealth and will
To instruct and teach? Or your unwearied pain
Of gathering? Bounty in pouring out again?
What fables have you vexed! What truth redeemed!
Antiquities searched! Opinions disesteemed!   40
Impostures branded! And authorities urged!
What blots and errors have you watched and purged
Records, and authors of! How rectified
Times, manners, customs! Innovations spied!
Sought out the fountains, sources, creeks, paths, ways,
And noted the beginnings and decays!
Where is that nominal mark, or real rite,
Form, act or ensign, that hath 'scaped your sight?
How are traditions there examined: how
Conjectures retrieved! And a story now   50
And then of times (besides the bare conduct
Of what it tells us) weaved in to instruct.
I wondered at the richness, but am lost,
To see the workmanship so exceed the cost!
To mark the excellent seasoning of your style!
And manly elocution, not one while
With horror rough, then rioting with wit!
But to the subject, still the colours fit
In sharpness of all search, wisdom of choice,
Newness of sense, antiquity of voice!   60
      I yield, I yield, the matter of your praise
Flows in upon me, and I cannot raise
A bank against it. Nothing but the round
Large clasp of nature, such a wit can bound.
Monarch in letters! 'Mongst thy titles shown
Of others' honours, thus, enjoy thine own.

I first salute thee so; and gratulate
With that thy style, thy keeping of thy state,
In offering this thy work to no great name,
70   That would, perhaps, have praised, and thanked the same,
But naught beyond. He thou hast given it to,
Thy learnèd chamber-fellow, knows to do
It true respects. He will not only love,
Embrace, and cherish; but he can approve
And estimate thy pains; as having wrought
In the same mines of knowledge; and thence brought
Humanity enough to be a friend,
And strength to be a champion, and defend
Thy gift 'gainst envy. O how I do count
80   Among my comings in, and see it mount,
The grain of your two friendships! Hayward and
Selden! Two names that so much understand!
On whom I could take up, and ne'er abuse
The credit, what would furnish a tenth muse!
But here's no time, nor place, my wealth to tell,
You both are modest. So am I. Farewell.

An Epistle to a Friend, to Persuade Him to the Wars

∞

Wake, friend, from forth thy lethargy: the drum
Beats brave, and loud in Europe, and bids come
All that dare rouse: or are not loth to quit
Their vicious ease, and be o'erwhelmed with it.
It is a call to keep the spirits alive
That gasp for action, and would yet revive
Man's buried honour, in his sleepy life:
Quickening dead nature, to her noblest strife.

All other acts of worldlings, are but toil
In dreams, begun in hope, and end in spoil.   10
Look on the ambitious man, and see him nurse
His unjust hopes, with praises begged, or (worse)
Bought flatteries, the issue of his purse,
Till he become both their, and his own curse!
Look on the false, and cunning man, that loves
No person, nor is loved: what ways he proves
To gain upon his belly; and at last
Crushed in the snaky brakes, that he had passed!
See, the grave, sour, and supercilious sir
In outward face, but inward, light as fur,   20
Or feathers: lay his fortune out to show
Till envy wound, or maim it at a blow!
See him, that's called, and thought the happiest man,
Honoured at once, and envied (if it can
Be honour is so mixed) by such as would
For all their spite be like him if they could:
No part or corner man can look upon,
But there are objects, bid him to be gone
As far as he can fly, or follow day,
Rather than here so bogged in vices stay.   30
The whole world here leavened with madness swells;
And being a thing, blown out of naught, rebels
Against his Maker; high alone with weeds,
And impious rankness of all sects and seeds:
Not to be checked, or frighted now with fate,
But more licentious made, and desperate!
Our delicacies are grown capital,
And even our sports are dangers! What we call
Friendship is now masked hatred! Justice fled,
And shamefastness together! All laws dead   40
That kept man living! Pleasures only sought!
Honour and honesty, as poor things thought
As they are made! Pride and stiff clownage mixed
To make up greatness! And man's whole good fixed
In bravery, or gluttony, or coin,
All which he makes the servants of the groin,

Thither it flows; how much did Stallion spend
To have his court-bred filly there commend
His lace and starch? And fall upon her back
50 In admiration, stretched upon the rack
Of lust, to his rich suit and title, Lord?
Aye, that's a charm and half! She must afford
That all respect; she must lie down: nay more,
'Tis there civility to be a whore;
He's one of blood, and fashion! And with these
The bravery makes, she can no honour leese:
To do it with cloth, or stuffs, lust's name might merit;
With velvet, plush, and tissues, it is spirit.

O, these so ignorant monsters! Light, as proud,
60 Who can behold their manners, and not cloud-
Like upon them lighten? If nature could
Not make a verse; anger; or laughter would
To see them aye discoursing with their glass,
How they may make someone that day an ass,
Planting their purls, and curls spread forth like net,
And every dressing for a pitfall set
To catch the flesh in, and to pound a prick;
Be at their visits, see them squeamish, sick,
Ready to cast, at one, whose band sits ill,
70 And then, leap mad on a neat pickardil,
As if a brise were gotten in their tail,
And firk, and jerk, and for the coachman rail,
And jealous each of other, yet think long
To be abroad chanting some bawdy song,
And laugh, and measure thighs, then squeak, spring, itch,
Do all the tricks of a saut lady bitch;
For t'other pound of sweetmeats, he shall feel
That pays, or what he will. The dame is steel,
For these with her young company she'll enter,
80 Where Pitts, or Wright, or Modet would not venter,
And comes by these degrees, the style t'inherit
Of woman of fashion, and a lady of spirit:
Nor is the title questioned with our proud,
Great, brave, and fashioned folk, these are allowed

Adulteries now, are not so hid, or strange,
They're grown commodity upon Exchange;
He that will follow but another's wife,
Is loved, though he let out his own for life:
The husband now's called churlish, or a poor
Nature, that will not let his wife be a whore;   90
Or use all arts, or haunt all companies
That may corrupt her, even in his eyes.
The brother trades a sister; and the friend
Lives to the lord, but to the lady's end.
Less must not be thought on than mistress: or
If it be thought, killed like her embrions; for,
Whom no great mistress hath as yet infamed
A fellow of coarse lechery, is named
The servant of the serving woman in scorn,
Ne'er came to taste the plenteous marriage horn.   100
    Thus they do talk. And are these objects fit
For man to spend his money on? His wit?
His time? Health? Soul? Will he for these go throw
Those thousands on his back, shall after blow
His body to the Counters, or the Fleet?
Is it for these that Fine-man meets the street
Coached, or on foot-cloth, thrice-changed every day?
To teach each suit, he has the ready way
From Hyde Park to the stage, where at the last
His dear and borrowed bravery he must cast;   110
When not his combs, his curling irons, his glass,
Sweet bags, sweet powders, nor sweet words will pass
For less security. O, friend, for these
Is it that man pulls on himself disease?
Surfeit? And quarrel? Drinks the tother health?
Or by damnation voids it? Or by stealth?
What fury of late is crept into our feasts?
What honour given to the drunkenest guests?
What reputation to bear one glass more?
When oft the bearer is borne out of door?   120
This hath our ill-used freedom, and soft peace
Brought on us, and will every hour increase.

Our vices do not tarry in a place,
But being in motion still (or rather in race)
Tilt one upon another, and now bear
This way, now that, as if their number were
More than themselves, or than our lives could take,
But both fell pressed under the load they make.
    I'll bid thee look no more, but flee, flee friend,
130 This precipice, and rocks, that have no end,
Or side, but threatens ruin. The whole day
Is not enough now, but the night's to play:
And whilst our states, strength, body, and mind we waste;
Go make ourselves the usurer's at a cast.
He that no more for age, cramps, palsies, can
Now use the bones, we see doth hire a man
To take the box up for him; and pursues
The dice with glassen eyes, to the glad views
Of what he throws: like lechers grown content
140 To be beholders, when their powers are spent.
    Can we not leave this worm? Or will we not?
Is that the truer excuse? Or have we got
In this, and like, an itch of vanity,
That scratching now's our best felicity?
Well, let it go. Yet this is better, than
To lose the forms, and dignities of men
To flatter my good lord, and cry his bowl
Runs sweetly, as it had his lordship's soul.
Although, perhaps it has, what's that to me,
150 That may stand by, and hold my peace? Will he
When I am hoarse, with praising his each cast,
Give me but that again, that I must waste
In sugar candied, or in buttered beer,
For the recovery of my voice? No, there
Pardon his lordship. Flattery's grown so cheap
With him, for he is followed with that heap
That watch, and catch, at what they may applaud,
As a poor single flatterer, without bawd,
Is nothing, such scarce meat and drink he'll give,
160 But he that's both, and slave to boot, shall live,

And he beloved, while the whores last. O times,
Friend fly from hence; and let these kindled rhymes
Light thee from hell on earth: where flatterers, spies,
Informers, masters both of arts and lies;
Lewd slanderers, soft whisperers that let blood
The life, and fame-veins (yet not understood
Of the poor sufferers); where the envious, proud,
Ambitious, factious, superstitious, loud
Boasters, and perjured, with the infinite more
Prevaricators swarm. Of which the store   170
(Because they are everywhere amongst mankind
Spread through the world) is easier far to find,
Than once to number, or bring forth to hand,
Though thou wert muster-master of the land.
   Go quit them all. And take along with thee,
Thy true friend's wishes, Colby, which shall be,
That thine be just, and honest, that thy deeds
Not wound thy conscience, when thy body bleeds;
That thou dost all things more for truth, than glory,
And never but for doing wrong be sorry;   180
That by commanding first thyself, thou mak'st
Thy person fit for any charge thou tak'st;
That fortune never make thee to complain,
But what she gives, thou dar'st give her again;
That whatsoever face thy fate puts on,
Thou shrink or start not; but be always one;
That thou think nothing great, but what is good,
And from that thought strive to be understood.
So, 'live or dead, thou wilt preserve a fame
Still precious, with the odour of thy name.   190
And last, blaspheme not; we did never hear
Man thought the valianter, 'cause he durst swear,
No more, than we should think a lord had had
More honour in him, 'cause we have known him mad:
These take, and now go seek thy peace in war:
Who falls for love of God, shall rise a star.

Epistle to a Friend

∽

They are not, sir, worst owers, that do pay
Debts when they can: good men may break their day,
And yet the noble nature never grudge;
'Tis then a crime, when the usurer is judge,
And he is not in friendship. Nothing there
Is done for gain: if't be 'tis not sincere.
Nor should I at this time protested be,
But that some greater names have broke with me,
And their words too; where I but break my band.
10 I add that 'but' because I understand
That as the lesser breach: for he that takes
Simply my band, his trust in me forsakes,
And looks unto the forfeit. If you be
Now so much friend, as you would trust in me,
Venter a longer time, and willingly:
All is not barren land, doth fallow lie.
Some grounds are made the richer, for the rest;
And I will bring a crop, if not the best.

An Elegy

∽

Can beauty that did prompt me first to write,
Now threaten, with those means she did invite?
Did her perfections call me on to gaze,
Then like, then love; and now would they amaze?
Or was she gracious afar off, but near
A terror? Or is all this but my fear?
That as the water makes things, put in't, straight,
Crookèd appear; so that doth my conceit:
I can help that with boldness; and love sware,
And fortune once, to assist the spirits that dare.   10
But which shall lead me on? Both these are blind:
Such guides men use not, who their way would find,
Except the way be error to those ends:
And then the best are, still, the blindest friends!
O how a lover may mistake! To think,
Or love, or fortune blind, when they but wink
To see men fear: or else for truth, and state,
Because they would free justice imitate,
Veil their own eyes, and would impartially
Be brought by us to meet our destiny.   20
If it be thus; come love, and fortune go,
I'll lead you on; or if my fate will so,
That I must send one first, my choice assigns,
Love to my heart, and fortune to my lines.

An Elegy

By those bright eyes, at whose immortal fires
Love lights his torches to inflame desires,
By that fair stand, your forehead, whence he bends
His double bow, and round his arrows sends;
By that tall grove, your hair; whose globy rings
He flying curls, and crispeth, with his wings;
By those pure baths your either cheek discloses,
Where he doth steep himself in milk and roses;
And lastly by your lips, the bank of kisses,
Where men at once may plant, and gather blisses:
Tell me (my loved friend) do you love or no?
So well as I may tell in verse, 'tis so?
You blush, but do not: friends are either none,
(Though they may number bodies) or but one.
I'll therefore ask no more, but bid you love;
And so that either may example prove
Unto the other; and live patterns, how
Others in time may love, as we do now.
Slip no occasion; as time stands not still,
I know no beauty, nor no youth that will.
To use the present, then, is not abuse;
You have a husband is the just excuse
Of all that can be done him; such a one
As would make shift, to make himself alone,
That which we can, who both in you, his wife,
His issue, and all circumstance of life,
As in his place, because he would not vary,
Is constant to be extraordinary.

An Ode

∞

High-spirited friend,
I send nor balms, nor corsives to your wound;
    Your fate hath found
A gentler, and more agile hand, to tend
The cure of that, which is but corporal,
And doubtful days (which were named critical),
    Have made their fairest flight,
    And now are out of sight.
Yet doth some wholesome physic for the mind,
    Wrapped in this paper lie,   10
Which in the taking if you misapply,
    You are unkind.

    Your covetous hand,
Happy in that fair honour it hath gained,
    Must now be reined.
True valour doth her own renown command
In one full action; nor have you now more
To do, than be a husband of that store.
    Think but how dear you bought
    This same which you have caught,   20
Such thoughts will make you more in love with truth:
    'Tis wisdom and that high,
For men to use their fortune reverently,
    Even in youth.

An Elegy

∞

'Tis true, I'm broke! Vows, oaths, and all I had
Of credit lost. And I am now run mad:
Or do upon myself some desperate ill;
This sadness makes no approaches, but to kill.
It is a darkness hath blocked up my sense,
And drives it in to eat on my offence,
Or there to starve it. Help, O you that may
Alone lend succours, and this fury stay.
Offended mistress, you are yet so fair,
10   As light breaks from you, that affrights despair,
And fills my powers with persuading joy,
That you should be too noble to destroy.
There may some face or menace of a storm
Look forth, but cannot last in such a form.
If there be nothing worthy you can see
Of graces, or your mercy here in me,
Spare your own goodness yet; and be not great
In will and power, only to defeat.
God, and the good, know to forgive, and save.
20   The ignorant, and fools, no pity have.
I will not stand to justify my fault,
Or lay the excuse upon the vintner's vault;
Or in confessing of the crime be nice,
Or go about to countenance the vice,
By naming in what company 'twas in,
As I would urge authority for sin.
No, I will stand arraigned, and cast, to be
The subject of your grace in pardoning me,
And (styled your mercy's creature) will live more
30   Your honour now, than your disgrace before.
Think it was frailty, mistress, think me man,
Think that yourself like heaven forgive me can:
Where weakness doth offend, and virtue grieve,

There greatness takes a glory to relieve.
Think that I once was yours, or may be now;
Nothing is vile, that is a part of you:
Error and folly in me may have crossed
Your just commands; yet those, not I be lost.
I am regenerate now, become the child
Of your compassion; parents should be mild: 40
There is no father that for one demerit,
Or two, or three, a son will disinherit –
That is the last of punishments is meant:
No man inflicts that pain, till hope be spent.
An ill-affected limb (whate'er it ail)
We cut not off, till all cures else do fail:
And then with pause; for severed once, that's gone,
Would live his glory that could keep it on;
Do not despair my mending; to distrust
Before you prove a medicine, is unjust.   50
You may so place me, and in such an air
As not alone the cure, but scar be fair.
That is, if still your favours you apply,
And not the bounties you have done, deny.
Could you demand the gifts you gave, again?
Why was it? Did e'er the clouds ask back their rain?
The sun his heat, and light, the air his dew?
Or winds the spirit, by which the flower so grew?
That were to wither all, and make a grave
Of that wise nature would a cradle have!   60
Her order is to cherish, and preserve,
Consumption's nature to destroy, and starve.
But to exact again what once is given,
Is nature's mere obliquity! As heaven
Should ask the blood, and spirits he hath infused
In man, because man hath the flesh abused.
O may your wisdom take example hence,
God lightens not at man's each frail offence,
He pardons slips, goes by a world of ills,
And then his thunder frights more, than it kills.   70
He cannot angry be, but all must quake,

It shakes even him, that all things else doth shake.
And how more fair, and lovely looks the world
In a calm sky; than when the heaven is hurled
About in clouds, and wrapped in raging weather,
As all with storm and tempest ran together.
O imitate that sweet serenity
That makes us live, not that which calls to die.
In dark, and sullen morns; do we not say
80   This looketh like an execution day?
And with the vulgar doth it not obtain
The name of cruel weather, storm, and rain?
Be not affected with these marks too much
Of cruelty, lest they do make you such.
But view the mildness of your Maker's state,
As I the penitent's here emulate:
He, when he sees a sorrow such as this,
Straight puts off all his anger, and doth kiss
The contrite soul, who hath no thought to win
90   Upon the hope to have another sin
Forgiven him; and in that line stand I,
Rather than once displease you more, to die,
To suffer tortures, scorn, and infamy,
What fools, and all their parasites can apply;
The wit of ale, and genius of the malt
Can pump for; or a libel without salt
Produce; though threatening with a coal, or chalk
On every wall, and sung where e'er I walk.
I number these as being of the chore
100 Of contumely, and urge a good man more
Than sword, or fire, or what is of the race
To carry noble danger in the face:
There is not any punishment, or pain,
A man should fly from, as he would disdain.
Then mistress, here, here let your rigour end,
And let your mercy make me ashamed t'offend.
I will no more abuse my vows to you,
Than I will study falsehood, to be true.
O, that you could but by dissection see

How much you are the better part of me!   110
How all my fibres by your spirit do move,
And that there is no life in me, but love.
You would be then most confident, that though
Public affairs command me now to go
Out of your eyes, and be awhile away;
Absence, or distance, shall not breed decay.
Your form shines here, here fixèd in my heart:
I may dilate myself, but not depart.
Others by common stars their courses run,
When I see you, then I do see my sun,   120
Till then 'tis all but darkness, that I have;
Rather than want your light, I wish a grave.

An Elegy

∞

That love's a bitter sweet, I ne'er conceive
Till the sour minute comes of taking leave,
And then I taste it. But as men drink up
In haste the bottom of a medicined cup,
And take some syrup after; so do I,
To put all relish from my memory
Of parting, drown it in the hope to meet
Shortly again: and make our absence sweet.
This makes me, mistress, that sometime by stealth
Under another name, I take your health;   10
And turn the ceremonies of those nights
I give, or owe my friends, into your rites,
But ever without blazon, or least shade
Of vows so sacred, and in silence made;
For though love thrive, and may grow up with cheer,
And free society, he's born elsewhere,
And must be bred, so to conceal his birth,

As neither wine do rack it out, or mirth.
Yet should the lover still be airy and light,
20   In all his actions rarified to sprite;
Not like a Midas shut up in himself,
And turning all he toucheth into pelf,
Keep in reserved in his dark-lantern face,
As if that excellent dulness were love's grace;
No, mistress, no, the open merry man
Moves like a sprightly river, and yet can
Keep secret in his channels what he breeds
'Bove all your standing waters, choked with weeds.
They look at best like cream bowls, and you soon
30   Shall find their depth: they're sounded with a spoon.
They may say grace, and for love's chaplains pass;
But the grave lover ever was an ass;
Is fixed upon one leg, and dares not come
Out with the other, for he's still at home;
Like the dull, wearied crane that (come on land)
Doth, while he keeps his watch, betray his stand.
Where he that knows will like a lapwing fly
Far from the nest, and so himself belie
To others, as he will deserve the trust
40   Due to that one, that doth believe him just.
And such your servant is, who vows to keep
The jewel of your name, as close as sleep
Can lock the sense up, or the heart a thought,
And never be by time, or folly brought,
Weakness of brain, or any charm of wine,
The sin of boast, or other countermine
(Made to blow up love's secrets) to discover
That article, may not become your lover:
Which in assurance to your breast I tell,
50   If I had writ no word, but 'dear', farewell.

An Elegy

Since you must go, and I must bid farewell,
Hear, mistress, your departing servant tell
What it is like: and do not think they can
Be idle words, though of a parting man;
It is as if a night should shade noon-day,
Or that the sun was here, but forced away;
And we were left under that hemisphere,
Where we must feel it dark for half a year.
What fate is this to change men's days and hours,
To shift their seasons, and destroy their powers!   10
Alas I have lost my heat, my blood, my prime,
Winter is come a quarter ere his time,
My health will leave me; and when you depart,
How shall I do, sweet mistress, for my heart?
You would restore it? No, that's worth a fear,
As if it were not worthy to be there:
O, keep it still; for it had rather be
Your sacrifice, than here remain with me.
And so I spare it. Come what can become
Of me, I'll softly tread unto my tomb;   20
Or like a ghost walk silent amongst men,
Till I may see both it and you again.

An Elegy

∾

Let me be what I am, as Virgil cold;
As Horace fat; or as Anacreon old;
No poet's verses yet did ever move,
Whose readers did not think he was in love.
Who shall forbid me then in rhythm to be
As light, and active as the youngest he
That from the muses' fountains doth endorse
His lines, and hourly sits the poet's horse?
Put on my ivy garland, let me see
10 Who frowns, who jealous is, who taxeth me.
Fathers and husbands, I do claim a right
In all that is called lovely: take my sight
Sooner than my affection from the fair.
No face, no hand, proportion, line, or air
Of beauty; but the muse hath interest in:
There is not worn that lace, purl, knot or pin,
But is the poet's matter: and he must
When he is furious, love, although not lust.
But then content, your daughters and your wives,
20 (If they be fair and worth it) have their lives
Made longer by our praises. Or, if not,
Wish, you had foul ones, and deformèd got;
Cursed in their cradles, or there changed by elves,
So to be sure you do enjoy yourselves.
Yet keep those up in sackcloth too, or leather,
For silk will draw some sneaking songster thither.
It is a rhyming age, and verses swarm
At every stall; the city cap's a charm.
But I who live, and have lived twenty year
30 Where I may handle silk, as free, and near,
As any mercer; or the whalebone man
That quilts those bodies, I have leave to span:
Have eaten with the beauties, and the wits,

And braveries of court, and felt their fits
Of love, and hate: and came so nigh to know
Whether their faces were their own, or no:
It is not likely I should now look down
Upon a velvet petticoat, or a gown,
Whose like I have known the tailor's wife put on
To do her husband's rites in, ere 'twere gone   40
Home to the customer: his lechery
Being, the best clothes still to preoccupy.
Put a coach-mare in tissue, must I horse
Her presently? Or leap thy wife of force,
When by thy sordid bounty she hath on,
A gown of that was the caparison?
So I might dote upon thy chairs, and stools
That are like clothed: must I be of those fools
Of race accounted, that no passion have
But when thy wife (as thou conceiv'st) is brave?   50
Then ope thy wardrobe, think me that poor groom
That from the footman, when he was become
An officer there, did make most solemn love,
To every petticoat he brushed, and glove
He did lay up, and would adore the shoe,
Or slipper was left off, and kiss it too,
Court every hanging gown, and after that,
Lift up some one, and do, I tell not what.
Thou didst tell me; and wert o'erjoyed to peep
In at a hole, and see these actions creep   60
From the poor wretch, which though he played in prose,
He would have done in verse, with any of those
Wrung on the withers, by lord Love's despite,
Had he had the faculty to read, and write!
Such songsters there are store of; witness he
That chanced the lace, laid on a smock, to see,
And straightway spent a sonnet; with that other
That (in pure madrigal) unto his mother
Commended the French hood, and scarlet gown
The Lady Mayoress passed in through the town,   70

Unto the Spittle sermon. O, what strange
Variety of silks were on the Exchange!
Or in Moorfields! This other night, sings one,
Another answers, 'Las those silks are none,
In smiling *l'envoy*, as he would deride
Any comparison had with his Cheapside.
And vouches both the pageant, and the day,
When not the shops, but windows do display
The stuffs, the velvets, plushes, fringes, lace,
80 And all the original riots of the place:
Let the poor fools enjoy their follies, love
A goat in velvet; or some block could move
Under that cover; an old midwife's hat!
Or a close-stool so cased; or any fat
Bawd, in a velvet scabbard! I envy
None of their pleasures! Nor will ask thee, why
Thou art jealous of thy wife's, or daughter's case:
More than of either's manners, wit, or face!

An Execration upon Vulcan

∞

And why to me this, thou lame lord of fire,
What had I done that might call on thine ire?
Or urge thy greedy flame, thus to devour
So many my years' labours in an hour?
I ne'er attempted, Vulcan, 'gainst thy life;
Nor made least line of love to thy loose wife;
Or in remembrance of thy affront, and scorn,
With clowns, and tradesmen, kept thee closed in horn.
'Twas Jupiter that hurled thee headlong down,
10 And Mars, that gave thee a lantern for a crown:
Was it because thou wert of old denied
By Jove to have Minerva for thy bride,

That since thou tak'st all envious care and pain,
To ruin any issue of the brain?
Had I wrote treason there, or heresy,
Imposture, witchcraft, charms, or blasphemy,
I had deserved, then, thy consuming looks,
Perhaps, to have been burnèd with my books.
But, on thy malice, tell me, didst thou spy
Any, least loose, or scurrile paper, lie   20
Concealed or kept there, that was fit to be,
By thy own vote, a sacrifice to thee?
Did I there wound the honours of the crown?
Or tax the glories of the church, and gown?
Itch to defame the state? Or brand the times?
Any myself most, in some self-boasting rhymes?
If none of these, then why this fire? Or find
A cause before; or leave me one behind.
Had I compiled from *Amadis de Gaul*,
The *Esplandians*, *Arthurs*, *Palmerins*, and all   30
The learnèd library of Don Quixote;
And so some goodlier monster had begot,
Or spun out riddles, and weaved fifty tomes
Of logogriphs, and curious palindromes,
Or pomped for those hard trifles anagrams,
Or eteostichs, or those finer flammes
Of eegs, and halberds, cradles, and a hearse,
A pair of scissors, and a comb in verse;
Acrostichs, and telestichs, on jump names,
Thou then hadst had some colour for thy flames,   40
On such my serious follies; but, thou'lt say,
There were some pieces of as base allay,
And as false stamp there; parcels of a play,
Fitter to see the firelight, than the day;
Adulterate monies, such as might not go:
Thou shouldst have stayed, till public fame said so.
She is the judge, thou executioner:
Or if thou needs wouldst trench upon her power,
Thou mightst have yet enjoyed thy cruelty
With some more thrift, and more variety: 50

Thou mightst have had me perish, piece by piece,
To light tobacco, or save roasted geese,
Singe capons, or poor pigs, dropping their eyes:
Condemned me to the ovens with the pies;
And so, have kept me dying a whole age,
Not ravished all hence in a minute's rage.
But that's a mark, whereof thy rites do boast,
To make consumption, ever, where thou go'st;
Had I foreknown of this thy least desire
60 To have held a triumph, or a feast of fire,
Especially in paper: that, that steam
Had tickled your large nostril: many a ream,
To redeem mine, I had sent in; enough,
Thou shouldst have cried, and all been proper stuff.
The *Talmud*, and the *Alcoran* had come,
With pieces of the *Legend*; the whole sum
Of errant knighthood, with the dames, and dwarfs;
The charmèd boats, and the enchanted wharfs;
The Tristrams, Lancelots, Turpins, and the Peers,
70 All the mad Rolands, and sweet Oliveers;
To Merlin's marvels, and his cabal's loss,
With the chimera of the Rosy-Cross,
Their seals, their characters, hermetic rings,
Their gem of riches, and bright stone, that brings
Invisibility, and strength, and tongues:
The art of kindling the true coal, by lungs;
With Nicholas Pasquil's *Meddle with your match*,
And the strong lines, that so the time do catch,
Or Captain Pamphlet's horse, and foot, that sally
80 Upon the Exchange, still out of Pope's Head Alley.
The weekly corrants, with Paul's seal; and all
The admired discourses of the prophet Ball:
These, hadst thou pleased either to dine, or sup,
Had made a meal for Vulcan to lick up.
But in my desk, what was there to excite
So ravenous, and vast an appetite?
I dare not say a body, but some parts
There were of search, and mastery in the arts.

All the old Venusine, in poetry,
And lighted by the Stagerite, could spy,   90
Was there made English: with the Grammar too,
To teach some that, their nurses could not do –
The purity of language; and among
The rest, my journey into Scotland sung,
With all the adventures; three books not afraid
To speak the fate of the Sicilian maid
To our own ladies; and in story there
Of our fifth Henry, eight of his nine year;
Wherein was oil, beside the succour spent,
Which noble Carew, Cotton, Selden lent: 100
And twice twelve years stored up humanity,
With humble gleanings in divinity;
After the Fathers, and those wiser guides
Whom faction had not drawn to study sides.
How in these ruins, Vulcan, thou dost lurk,
All soot, and embers! Odious, as thy work!
I now begin to doubt, if ever grace,
Or goddess, could be patient of thy face.
Thou woo Minerva! Or to wit aspire!
'Cause thou canst halt, with us, in arts, and fire!   110
Son of the wind! For so thy mother gone
With lust conceived thee; father thou hadst none:
When thou wert born, and that thou look'st at best,
She durst not kiss, but flung thee from her breast.
And so did Jove, who ne'er meant thee his cup:
No mar'l the clowns of Lemnos took thee up,
For none but smiths would have made thee a god.
Some alchemist there may be yet, or odd
Squire of the squibs, against the pageant day,
May to thy name a Vulcanale say;   120
And for it lose his eyes with gunpowder,
As the other may his brains with quicksilver.
Well fare the wise men yet, on the Bankside,
My friends, the watermen! They could provide
Against thy fury, when to serve their needs,
They made a Vulcan of a sheaf of reeds,

Whom they durst handle in their holiday coats,
And safely trust to dress, not burn their boats.
But, O those reeds! Thy mere disdain of them,
130 Made thee beget that cruel stratagem,
(Which, some are pleased to style but thy mad prank)
Against the Globe, the glory of the Bank,
Which, though it were the fort of the whole parish,
Flanked with a ditch, and forced out of a marish,
I saw with two poor chambers taken in
And razed; ere thought could urge, this might have been!
See the world's ruins! Nothing but the piles
Left! And wit since to cover it with tiles.
The Brethren, they straight noised it out for news,
140 'Twas verily some relic of the stews:
And this a sparkle of that fire let loose
That was locked up in the Winchestrian goose
Bred on the Bank, in time of popery,
When Venus there maintained the mystery.
But, others fell, with that conceit by the ears,
And cried, it was a threatening to the bears;
And that accursèd ground, the Parish Garden:
Nay (sighed a sister) 'twas the nun, Kate Arden,
Kindled the fire! But, then did one return,
150 No fool would his own harvest spoil, or burn!
If that were so, thou rather wouldst advance
The place, that was thy wife's inheritance.
O no, cried all. Fortune, for being a whore,
Scaped not his justice any jot the more:
He burnt that idol of the Revels too:
Nay, let Whitehall with Revels have to do,
Though but in dances, it shall know his power;
There was a judgement shown too in an hour.
He is true Vulcan still! He did not spare
160 Troy, though it were so much his Venus' care.
Fool, wilt thou let that in example come?
Did she not save from thence, to build a Rome?
And what hast thou done in these petty spites,
More than advanced the houses, and their rites?

I will not argue thee, from those of guilt,
For they were burnt, but to be better built.
'Tis true, that in thy wish they were destroyed,
Which thou hast only vented, not enjoyed.
So wouldst thou have run upon the Rolls by stealth,
And didst invade part of the Commonwealth,   170
In those records, which were all chronicles gone,
Will be remembered by six clerks, to one.
But, say all six, good men, what answer ye?
Lies there no writ, out of the Chancery,
Against this Vulcan? No injunction?
No order? No decree? Though we be gone
At Common Law: methinks in his despite
A court of Equity should do us right,
But to confine him to the brew-houses,
The glasshouse, dye-fats, and their furnaces;   180
To live in sea coal, and go forth in smoke;
Or lest that vapour might the city choke,
Condemn him to the brick kilns, or some hill-
Foot (out in Sussex) to an iron mill;
Or in small faggots have him blaze about
Vile taverns, and the drunkards piss him out;
Or in the bellman's lantern, like a spy,
Burn to a snuff, and then stink out, and die:
I could invent a sentence, yet were worse;
But I'll conclude all in a civil curse.   190
Pox on your flameship, Vulcan; if it be
To all as fatal as't hath been to me,
And to Paul's steeple; which was unto us
'Bove all your fireworks had at Ephesus,
Or Alexandria; and though a divine
Loss remains yet, as unrepaired as mine.
Would you had kept your forge, at Etna still,
And there made swords, bills, glaives, and arms your fill;
Maintained the trade at Bilbo; or elsewhere;
Struck in at Milan with the cutlers there;   200
Or stayed but where the friar, and you first met,
Who from the devil's arse did guns beget;

Or fixed in the Low Countries, where you might
On both sides do your mischiefs with delight;
Blow up, and ruin, mine, and countermine,
Make your petards, and granats, all your fine
Engines of murder, and receive the praise
Of massacring mankind so many ways.
We ask your absence here, we all love peace,
210 And pray the fruits thereof, and the increase;
So doth the king, and most of the king's men
That have good places: therefore once again,
Pox on thee, Vulcan, thy Pandora's pox,
And all the evils that flew out of her box
Light on thee: or if those plagues will not do,
Thy wife's pox on thee, and Bess Braughton's too.

A Speech according to Horace

∞

Why yet, my noble hearts, they cannot say,
But we have powder still for the king's day,
And ordinance too: so much as from the tower
To have waked, if sleeping, Spain's ambassador,
Old Aesop Gondomar: the French can tell,
For they did see it the last tilting well,
That we have trumpets, armour, and great horse,
Lances, and men, and some a breaking force.
They saw too store of feathers, and more may,
10 If they stay here, but till Saint George's Day.
All ensigns of a war are not yet dead,
Nor marks of wealth so from our nation fled,
But they may see gold chains, and pearl worn then,
Lent by the London dames, to the lords' men;

Withal, the dirty pains those citizens take,
To see the pride at court, their wives do make:
And the return those thankful courtiers yield
To have their husbands drawn forth to the field,
And coming home, to tell what acts were done
Under the auspice of young Swinnerton.   20
What a strong fort old Pimlico had been!
How it held out! How (last) 'twas taken in!
Well, I say thrive, thrive brave Artillery vard,
Thou seed-plot of the war, that hast not spared
Powder, or paper, to bring up the youth
Of London, in the military truth,
These ten years' day; as all may swear that look
But on thy practice, and the posture book:
He that but saw thy curious captain's drill,
Would think no more of Flushing, or the Brill: 30
But give them over to the common ear
For that unnecessary charge they were.
Well did thy crafty clerk, and knight, Sir Hugh
Supplant bold Panton; and brought there to view
Translated Aelian *Tactics* to be read.
And the Greek discipline (with the modern) shed
So, in that ground as soon it grew to be
The city-question, whether Tilly, or he,
Were now the greater captain! For they saw
The Berghen siege, and taking in Breda,   40
So acted to the life, as Maurice might,
And Spinola have blushèd at the sight.
O happy art! And wise epitome
Of bearing arms! Most civil soldiery!
Thou canst draw forth thy forces, and fight dry
The battles of thy aldermanity;
Without the hazard of a drop of blood:
More than the surfeits, in thee, that day stood.
Go on, increase in virtue and in fame:
And keep the glory of the English name,   50
Up among nations. In the stead of bold
Beauchamps, and Nevills, Cliffords, Audleys old;

Insert thy Hodges, and those newer men,
As Stiles, Dike, Ditchfield, Millar, Crips, and Fen:
That keep the war, though now't be grown more tame,
Alive yet, in the noise; and still the same;
And could (if our great men would let their sons
Come to their schools) show them the use of guns.
And there instruct the noble English heirs
60   In politic and militar' affairs;
But he that should persuade, to have this done
For education of our lordings; soon
Should he not hear of billow, wind, and storm,
From the tempestuous grandlings? 'Who'll inform
Us, in our bearing, that are thus, and thus,
Born, bred, allied! What's he dare tutor us?
Are we by bookworms to be awed? Must we
Live by their scale, that dare do nothing free?
Why are we rich, or great, except to show
70   All licence in our lives? What need we know?
More than to praise a dog or horse? Or speak
The hawking language? Or our day to break
With citizens? Let clowns, and tradesmen breed
Their sons to study arts, the laws, the creed:
We will believe, like men of our own rank,
In so much land a year, or such a bank,
That turns us so much monies, at which rate
Our ancestors imposed on prince and state.
Let poor nobility be virtuous: we,
80   Descended in a rope of titles, be
From Guy, or Bevis, Arthur, or from whom
The herald will. Our blood is now become
Past any need of virtue. Let them care,
That in the cradle of their gentry are,
To serve the state by councils, and by arms:
We neither love the troubles, nor the harms.'
What love you then? Your whore? What study? Gait,
Carriage, and dressing? There is up of late
The academy, where the gallants meet –
90   What, to make legs? Yes, and to smell most sweet.

All that they do at plays. O, but first here
They learn and study; and then practise there.
But why are all these irons in the fire
Of several makings? Helps, helps, to attire
His lordship. That is for his band, his hair
This, and that box his beauty to repair;
This other for his eyebrows; hence, away,
I may no longer on these pictures stay,
These carcasses of honour; tailors' blocks,
Covered with tissue, whose prosperity mocks   100
The fate of things: whilst tottered virtue holds
Her broken arms up, to their empty moulds.

An Epistle answering to One that Asked to be Sealed of the Tribe of Ben

∞

Men that are safe, and sure, in all they do,
Care not what trials they are put unto;
They meet the fire, the test, as martyrs would;
And though opinion stamp them not, are gold.
I could say more of such, but that I fly
To speak myself out too ambitiously,
And showing so weak an act to vulgar eyes,
Put conscience and my right to compromise.
Let those that merely talk, and never think,
That live in the wild anarchy of drink   10
Subject to quarrel only; or else such
As make it their proficiency, how much
They have glutted in, and lechered out that week,
That never yet did friend, or friendship seek
But for a sealing: let these men protest.
Or the other on their borders, that will jest

On all souls that are absent: even the dead;
Like flies, or worms, which man's corrupt parts fed:
That to speak well, think it above all sin,
20 Of any company but that they are in,
Call every night to supper in these fits,
And are received for the covy of wits;
That censure all the town, and all the affairs,
And know whose ignorance is more than theirs;
Let these men have their ways, and take their times
To vent their libels, and to issue rhymes:
I have no portion in them, nor their deal
Of news they get, to strew out the long meal.
I study other friendships, and more one,
30 Than these can ever be; or else wish none.
What is't to me whether the French design
Be, or be not, to get the Valtelline?
Or the States' ships sent forth belike to meet
Some hopes of Spain in their West Indian fleet?
Whether the dispensation yet be sent,
Or that the match from Spain was ever meant?
I wish all well, and pray high heaven conspire
My prince's safety, and my king's desire,
But if for honour, we must draw the sword,
40 And force back that, which will not be restored,
I have a body, yet, that spirit draws
To live, or fall, a carcass in the cause.
So far without inquiry what the States,
Brunsfield, and Mansfield do this year, my fates
Shall carry me at call; and I'll be well,
Though I do neither hear these news, nor tell
Of Spain or France; or were not pricked down one
Of the late mystery of reception,
Although my fame, to his, not underhears,
50 That guides the motions, and directs the bears.
But that's a blow, by which in time I may
Lose all my credit with my Christmas clay,
And animated porcelain of the court;
Ay, and for this neglect, the coarser sort

Of earthen jars, there may molest me too:
Well, with mine own frail pitcher, what to do
I have decreed; keep it from waves, and press;
Lest it be jostled, cracked, made naught, or less:
Live to that point I will, for which I am man,
And dwell as in my centre, as I can,   60
Still looking to, and ever loving heaven;
With reverence using all the gifts thence given.
'Mongst which, if I have any friendships sent
Such as are square, well-tagged, and permanent,
Not built with canvas, paper, and false lights
As are the glorious scenes, at the great sights;
And that there be no fevery heats, nor colds,
Oily expansions, or shrunk dirty folds,
But all so clear, and led by reason's flame,
As but to stumble in her sight were shame.   70
These I will honour, love, embrace, and serve:
And free it from all question to preserve.
So short you read my character, and theirs
I would call mine, to which not many stairs
Are asked to climb. First give me faith, who know
Myself a little. I will take you so,
As you have writ yourself. Now stand, and then,
Sir, you are sealèd of the tribe of Ben.

An Epigram on the Court Pucell

∞

Does the court pucell then so censure me,
And thinks I dare not her? Let the world see.
What though her chamber be the very pit
Where fight the prime cocks of the game, for wit?
And that as any are struck, her breath creates
New in their stead, out of the candidates?

What though with tribade lust she force a muse,
And in an epicoene fury can write news
Equal with that, which for the best news goes,
As airy light, and as like wit as those?
What though she talk, and cannot once with them
Make state, religion, bawdry, all a theme?
And as lip-thirsty, in each word's expense,
Doth labour with the phrase more than the sense?
What though she ride two mile on holidays
To church, as others do to feasts and plays,
To show their tires? To view, and to be viewed?
What though she be with velvet gowns endued,
And spangled petticoats brought forth to eye,
As new rewards of her old secrecy?
What though she hath won on trust, as many do,
And that her truster fears her? Must I too?
I never stood for any place: my wit
Thinks itself naught, though she should value it.
I am no statesman, and much less divine;
For bawdry, 'tis her language, and not mine.
Farthest I am from the idolatry
To stuffs and laces, those my man can buy.
And trust her I would least, that hath forswore
In contract twice; what can she perjure more?
Indeed, her dressing some man might delight,
Her face there's none can like by candle-light.
Not he, that should the body have, for case
To his poor instrument, now out of grace.
Shall I advise thee, pucell? Steal away
From court, while yet thy fame hath some small day;
The wits will leave you, if they once perceive
You cling to lords; and lords, if them you leave
For sermoneers: of which now one, now other,
They say you weekly invite with fits o'th'mother,
And practise for a miracle; take heed,
This age would lend no faith to Dorrel's deed.
Or if it would, the court is the worst place,
Both for the mothers and the babes of grace,

For there the wicked in the chair of scorn,
Will call it a bastard, when a prophet's born.

(*A Poem Sent Me by Sir William Burlase*)

∽

THE PAINTER TO THE POET

To paint thy worth, if rightly I did know it,
And were but painter half like thee, a poet;
     Ben, I would show it:
But in this skill, my unskilful pen will tire,
Thou, and thy worth, will still be found far higher;
     And I a liar.
Then, what a painter's here? Or what an eater
Of great attempts? When as his skill's no greater,
     And he a cheater?
Then what a poet's here? Whom, by confession   10
Of all with me, to paint without digression
     There's no expression.

My Answer

THE POET TO THE PAINTER

Why? Though I seem of a prodigious waist,
I am not so voluminous, and vast,
But there are lines, wherewith I might be embraced.

'Tis true, as my womb swells, so my back stoops,
And the whole lump grows round, deformed, and droops,
But yet the tun at Heidelberg had hoops.

You were not tied, by any painter's law
To square my circle, I confess; but draw
My superficies: that was all you saw.

10   Which if in compass of no art it came
To be describèd by a monogram,
With one great blot, you had formed me as I am.

But whilst you curious were to have it be
An archetype, for all the world to see,
You made it a brave piece, but not like me.

O, had I now your manner, mastery, might,
Your power of handling shadow, air, and sprite,
How I would draw, and take hold, and delight.

But, you are he can paint; I can but write:
20   A poet hath no more but black and white,
Ne knows he flattering colours, or false light.

Yet when of friendship I would draw the face,
A lettered mind, and a large heart would place
To all posterity; I will write *Burlase*.

To Master John Burges

∞

Father John Burges,
Necessity urges
My woeful cry,
To Sir Robert Pie:
And that he will venter
To send my debentur.
Tell him his Ben
Knew the time, when

He loved the muses;
Though now he refuses   10
To take apprehension
Of a year's pension,
And more is behind:
Put him in mind
Christmas is near;
And neither good cheer,
Mirth, fooling, nor wit,
Nor any least fit
Of gambol, or sport
Will come at the court.   20
If there be no money,
No plover, or cony
Will come to the table,
Or wine to enable
The muse, or the poet,
The parish will know it.
Nor any quick-warming pan help him to bed,
If the 'chequer be empty, so will be his head.

An Epigram. To William, Earl of Newcastle

∽

They talk of fencing, and the use of arms,
The art of urging, and avoiding harms,
The noble science, and the mastering skill
Of making just approaches how to kill:
To hit in angles, and to clash with time;
As all defence, or óffence were a chime!
I hate such measured, give me mettled fire
That trembles in the blaze, but (then) mounts higher!
A quick, and dazzling motion! When a pair

10 Of bodies meet like rarified air!
Their weapons shot out, with that flame, and force,
As they outdid the lightning in the course;
This were a spectacle! A sight to draw
Wonder to valour! No, it is the law
Of daring, not to do a wrong is true
Valour! To slight it, being done to you!
To know the heads of danger! Where 'tis fit
To bend, to break, provoke, or suffer it!
All this (my lord) is valour! This is yours!
20 And was your father's! All your ancestors!
Who durst live great, 'mongst all the colds, and heats,
Of human life! As all the frosts, and sweats
Of fortune! When, or death appeared, or bands!
And valiant were, with, or without their hands.

An Epigram.
To K[ing] Charles for a Hundred Pounds
He Sent Me in My Sickness. 1629

∞

Great Charles, among the holy gifts of grace
Annexéd to thy person, and thy place,
'Tis not enough (thy piety is such)
To cure the called King's evil with thy touch;
But thou wilt yet a kinglier mastery try,
To cure the poet's evil, poverty:
And, in these cures, dost so thyself enlarge,
As thou dost cure our evil, at thy charge.
Nay, and in this, thou show'st to value more
10 One poet, than of other folk ten score.
O piety! So to weigh the poor's estates!
O bounty! So to difference the rates!

What can the poet wish his king may do,
But, that he cure the people's evil too?

An Ode, or Song, by All the Muses

∞

IN CELEBRATION OF HER
MAJESTY'S BIRTHDAY. 1630

1 CLIO.
Up public joy, remember
This sixteenth of November,
 Some brave uncommon way:
And though the parish steeple
Be silent, to the people
 Ring thou it holiday.

2 MEL.
What, though the thrifty tower
And guns there, spare to pour
 Their noises forth in thunder:
As fearful to awake   10
This city, or to shake
 Their guarded gates asunder?

3 THAL.
Yet, let our trumpets sound;
And cleave both air and ground,
 With beating of our drums:
Let every lyre be strung,
Harp, lute, theorbo sprung,
 With touch of dainty thumbs!

4 EUT.

That when the choir is full,
20   The harmony may pull
    The angels from their spheres:
And each intelligence
May wish itself a sense,
    Whilst it the ditty hears.

5 TERP.

Behold the royal Mary,
The daughter of great Harry!
    And sister to just Lewis!
Comes in the pomp, and glory
Of all her brother's story,
30   And of her father's prowess!

6 ERAT.

She shows so far above
The feignèd queen of love,
    This sea-girt isle upon:
As here no Venus were;
But, that she reigning here,
    Had got the Ceston on!

7 CALLI.

See, see our active king
Hath taken twice the ring
    Upon his pointed lance:
40 Whilst all the ravished rout
Do mingle in a shout,
    Hey! for the flower of France!

8 URA.

This day the court doth measure
Her joy in state, and pleasure;
    And with a reverend fear,
The revels, and the play,
Sum up this crownèd day,
    Her two and twentieth year!

138

9 POLY.
Sweet happy Mary! All
The people her do call!   50
    And this the womb divine!
So fruitful and so fair,
Hath brought the land an heir!
    And Charles a Caroline!

To the Immortal Memory and Friendship of that Noble Pair, Sir Lucius Cary and Sir H. Morison

∞

THE TURN

Brave infant of Saguntum, clear
Thy coming forth in that great year,
When the prodigious Hannibal did crown
His rage, with razing your immortal town.
Thou looking then about,
Ere thou wert half got out,
Wise child, didst hastily return,
And mad'st thy mother's womb thine urn.
How summed a circle didst thou leave mankind
Of deepest lore, could we the centre find!   10

THE COUNTER-TURN

Did wiser nature draw thee back,
From out the horror of that sack,
Where shame, faith, honour, and regard of right
Lay trampled on; the deeds of death, and night,
Urged, hurried forth, and hurled
Upon the affrighted world:

Sword, fire, and famine, with fell fury met;
And all on utmost ruin set;
As, could they but life's miseries foresee,
20   No doubt all infants would return like thee?

THE STAND
For, what is life, if measured by the space,
Not by the act?
Or maskèd man, if valued by his face,
Above his fact?
Here's one outlived his peers,
And told forth fourscore years;
He vexèd time, and busied the whole state;
Troubled both foes, and friends;
But ever to no ends:
30   What did this stirrer, but die late?
How well at twenty had he fallen, or stood!
For three of his four score, he did no good.

THE TURN
He entered well, by virtuous parts,
Got up and thrived with honest arts:
He purchased friends, and fame, and honours then,
And had his noble name advanced with men:
But weary of that flight,
He stooped in all men's sight
To sordid flatteries, acts of strife,
40   And sunk in that dead sea of life
So deep, as he did then death's waters sup;
But that the cork of title buoyed him up.

THE COUNTER-TURN
Alas, but Morison fell young:
He never fell, thou fall'st, my tongue.
He stood, a soldier to the last right end,
A perfect patriot, and a noble friend,
But most a virtuous son.
All offices were done
By him, so ample, full, and round,

In weight, in measure, number, sound,   50
As though his age imperfect might appear,
His life was of humanity the sphere.

THE STAND

Go now, and tell out days summed up with fears,
And make them years;
Produce thy mass of miseries on the stage,
To swell thine age:
Repeat of things a throng,
To show thou hast been long,
Not lived; for life doth her great actions spell,
By what was done and wrought   60
In season, and so brought
To light: her measures are, how well
Each syllabe answered, and was formed, how fair;
These make the lines of life, and that's her air.

THE TURN

It is not growing like a tree
In bulk, doth make man better be;
Or standing long an oak, three hundred year,
To fall a log, at last, dry, bald, and sere:
A lily of a day,
Is fairer far, in May,   70
Although it fall, and die that night;
It was the plant, and flower of light.
In small proportions, we just beauties see:
And in short measures, life may perfect be.

THE COUNTER-TURN

Call, noble Lucius, then for wine,
And let thy looks with gladness shine:
Accept this garland, plant it on thy head,
And think, nay know, thy Morison's not dead.
He leapt the present age,
Possessed with holy rage,   80
To see that bright eternal day:
Of which we priests, and poets say

Such truths, as we expect for happy men,
And there he lives with memory: and Ben

THE STAND

Jonson! Who sung this of him, ere he went
Himself to rest,
Or taste a part of that full joy he meant
To have expressed,
In this bright asterism:
90   Where it were friendship's schism,
(Were not his Lucius long with us to tarry)
To separate these twi-
Lights, the Dioscuri;
And keep the one half from his Harry.
But fate doth so alternate the design,
Whilst that in heaven, this light on earth must shine.

THE TURN

And shine as you exalted are;
Two names of friendship, but one star:
Of hearts the union. And those not by chance
100   Made, or indenture, or leased out to advance
The profits for a time.
No pleasures vain did chime,
Of rhymes, or riots, at your feasts,
Orgies of drink, or feigned protests:
But simple love of greatness, and of good;
That knits brave minds, and manners, more than
    blood.

THE COUNTER-TURN

This made you first to know the why
You liked, then after, to apply
That liking; and approach so one the tother,
110   Till either grew a portion of the other:
Each stylèd by his end,
The copy of his friend.
You lived to be the great surnames,
And titles, by which all made claims

Unto the virtue. Nothing perfect done,
But as a Cary, or a Morison.

THE STAND
And such a force the fair example had,
As they that saw
The good, and durst not practise it, were glad
That such a law   120
Was left yet to mankind;
Where they might read, and find
Friendship, in deed, was written, not in words:
And with the heart, not pen,
Of two so early men,
Whose lines her rolls were, and records,
Who, ere the first down bloomèd on the chin,
Had sowed these fruits, and got the harvest in.

*To the Right Honourable, the Lord High
Treasurer of England. An Epistle Mendicant.*
1631
∞

My lord;
Poor wretched states, pressed by extremities,
Are fain to seek for succours, and supplies
Of princes' aids, or good men's charities.

Disease, the enemy, and his engineers,
Wants, with the rest of his concealed compeers,
Have cast a trench about me, now five years.

And made those strong approaches, by false braies,
Reducts, half-moons, horn-works, and such close ways,
The muse not peeps out, one of hundred days;

10 But lies blocked up, and straitened, narrowed in,
Fixed to the bed, and boards, unlike to win
Health, or scarce breath, as she had never bin.

Unless some saving honour of the crown,
Dare think it, to relieve, no less renown,
A bedrid wit, than a besiegèd town.

MISCELLANEOUS POEMS

❦

To the Reader

∞

This figure, that thou here seest put,
It was for gentle Shakespeare cut;
Wherein the graver had a strife
With nature, to outdo the life:
O, could he but have drawn his wit
As well in brass, as he hath hit
His face; the print would then surpass
All, that was ever writ in brass.
But, since he cannot, reader, look
Not on his picture, but his book.   10

To the Memory of My Beloved, the Author Mr William Shakespeare: And What He Hath Left Us

∞

To draw no envy (Shakespeare) on thy name,
Am I thus ample to thy book, and fame:
While I confess thy writings to be such,
As neither man, nor muse, can praise too much.
'Tis true, and all men's suffrage. But these ways
Were not the paths I meant unto thy praise:

For seeliest ignorance on these may light,
Which, when it sounds at best, but echoes right;
Or blind affection, which doth ne'er advance
10 The truth, but gropes, and urgeth all by chance;
Or crafty malice, might pretend this praise,
And think to ruin, where it seemed to raise.
These are, as some infamous bawd, or whore,
Should praise a matron. What could hurt her more?
But thou art proof against them, and indeed
Above the ill fortune of them, or the need.
I therefore will begin. Soul of the age!
The applause, delight, the wonder of our stage!
My Shakespeare, rise; I will not lodge thee by
20 Chaucer, or Spenser, or bid Beaumont lie
A little further, to make thee a room:
Thou art a monument, without a tomb,
And art alive still, while thy book doth live,
And we have wits to read, and praise to give.
That I not mix thee so, my brain excuses;
I mean with great, but disproportioned muses:
For, if I thought my judgement were of years,
I should commit thee surely with thy peers,
And tell, how far thou didst our Lyly outshine,
30 Or sporting Kyd, or Marlowe's mighty line.
And though thou hadst small Latin, and less Greek,
From thence to honour thee, I would not seek
For names; but call forth thundering Aeschylus,
Euripides, and Sophocles to us,
Pacuvius, Accius, him of Cordova dead,
To life again, to hear thy buskin tread,
And shake a stage: or, when thy socks were on,
Leave thee alone, for the comparison
Of all that insolent Greece, or haughty Rome
40 Sent forth, or since did from their ashes come.
Triumph, my Britain, thou hast one to show,
To whom all scenes of Europe homage owe.
He was not of an age, but for all time!
And all the muses still were in their prime,

When like Apollo he came forth to warm
Our ears, or like a Mercury to charm!
Nature herself was proud of his designs,
And joyed to wear the dressing of his lines!
Which were so richly spun, and woven so fit,
As, since, she will vouchsafe no other wit.   50
The merry Greek, tart Aristophanes,
Neat Terence, witty Plautus, now not please;
But antiquated, and deserted lie
As they were not of nature's family.
Yet must I not give nature all: thy art,
My gentle Shakespeare, must enjoy a part.
For though the poet's matter, nature be,
His art doth give the fashion. And, that he,
Who casts to write a living line, must sweat,
(Such as thine are) and strike the second heat   60
Upon the muses' anvil: turn the same,
(And himself with it) that he thinks to frame;
Or for the laurel, he may gain a scorn,
For a good poet's made, as well as born.
And such wert thou. Look how the father's face
Lives in his issue, even so, the race
Of Shakespeare's mind, and manners brightly shines
In his well-turnéd, and true filéd lines:
In each of which, he seems to shake a lance,
As brandished at the eyes of ignorance.   70
Sweet swan of Avon, what a sight it were
To see thee in our waters yet appear,
And make those flights upon the banks of Thames,
That so did take Eliza, and our James!
But stay, I see thee in the hemisphere
Advanced, and made a constellation there!
Shine forth, thou star of poets, and with rage,
Or influence, chide, or cheer the drooping stage;
Which, since thy flight from hence, hath mourned
   like night.
And despairs day, but for thy volume's light.   80

The Vision of Ben Jonson, on the Muses of His Friend M. Drayton

It hath been questioned, Michael, if I be
A friend at all; or, if at all, to thee:
Because, who make the question, have not seen
Those ambling visits, pass in verse, between
Thy muse, and mine, as they expect. 'Tis true:
You have not writ to me, nor I to you;
And, though I now begin, 'tis not to rub
Hanch against hanch, or raise a rhyming club
About the town: this reckoning I will pay,
10   Without conferring symbols. This is my day.

   It was no dream! I was awake, and saw!
Lend me thy voice, O Fame, that I may draw
Wonder to truth, and have my vision hurled,
Hot from thy trumpet, round about the world.

   I saw a beauty from the sea to rise,
That all earth looked on; and that earth, all eyes!
It cast a beam as when the cheerful sun
Is fair got up, and day some hours begun,
And filled an orb as circular, as heaven!
20   The orb was cut forth into regions seven,
And those so sweet, and well-proportioned parts,
As it had been the circle of the arts!
When, by thy bright *Ideas* standing by,
I found it pure, and perfect poesy,
There read I, straight, thy learnèd *Legends* three,
Heard the soft airs, between our swains and thee,
Which made me think, the old Theocritus,
Or rural Virgil come, to pipe to us!
But then, thy epistolar *Heroic Songs*,
30   Their loves, their quarrels, jealousies, and wrongs,
Did all so strike me, as I cried, who can

With us be called, the Naso, but this man?
And looking up, I saw Minerva's fowl,
Perched overhead, the wise Athenian *Owl*:
I thought thee then our Orpheus, that wouldst try
Like him, to make the air, one volary:
And I had styled thee, Orpheus, but before
My lips could form the voice, I heard that roar,
And rouse, the marching of a mighty force,
Drums against drums, the neighing of the horse,   40
The fights, the cries; and wondering at the jars
I saw, and read, it was thy *Barons' Wars*!
O, how in those, dost thou instruct these times,
That rebels' actions, are but valiant crimes!
And carried, though with shout, and noise, confess
A wild, and an authorized wickedness!
Say'st thou so, Lucan? But thou scorn'st to stay
Under one title. Thou hast made thy way
And flight about the isle, well near, by this,
In thy admired periegesis,   50
Or universal circumduction
Of all that read thy *Poly-Olbion*.
That read it? That are ravished! Such was I
With every song, I swear, and so would die;
But that I hear, again, thy drum to beat
A better cause, and strike the bravest heat
That ever yet did fire the English blood!
Our right in France, if rightly understood:
There, thou art Homer! Pray thee, use the style
Thou hast deserved: and let me read the while   60
Thy catalogue of ships, exceeding his,
Thy list of aids, and force, for so it is:
The poet's act! And for his country's sake
Brave are the musters, that the muse will make.
And when he ships them where to use their arms,
How do his trumpets breathe! What loud alarms!
Look, how we read the Spartans were inflamed
With bold Tyrtaeus' verse, when thou art named,
So shall our English youth urge on, and cry

70 An *Agincourt*, an *Agincourt*, or die.
This book! It is a catechism to fight,
And will be bought of every lord, and knight,
That can but read; who cannot, may in prose
Get broken pieces, and fight well by those.
The miseries of Margaret the queen
Of tender eyes will more be wept, than seen:
I feel it by mine own, that overflow,
And stop my sight, in every line I go.
But then refreshèd, with thy *Fairy Court*,

80 I look on *Cynthia*, and *Sirena*'s sport,
As, on two flowery carpets, that did rise,
And with their grassy green restored mine eyes.
Yet give me leave, to wonder at the birth
Of thy strange *Moon Calf*, both thy strain of mirth,
And gossip-got acquaintance, as, to us
Thou hadst brought Lapland, or old Cobalus,
Empusa, Lamia, or some monster, more
Than Afric knew, or the full Grecian store!
I gratulate it to thee, and thy ends,

90 To all thy virtuous, and well-chosen friends,
Only my loss is, that I am not there:
And, till I worthy am to wish I were,
I call the world, that envies me, to see
If I can be a friend, and friend to thee.

Ode to Himself

Come leave the loathèd stage,
    And the more loathsome age,
Where pride and impudence in faction knit,
    Usurp the chair of wit:
Indicting and arraigning every day,
    Something they call a play.
    Let their fastidious, vain
    Commission of the brain,
Run on, and rage, sweat, censure, and condemn:
They were not made for thee, less thou for them.   10

Say that thou pour'st them wheat,
    And they would acorns eat:
'Twere simple fury, still thyself to waste
    On such as have no taste:
To offer them a surfeit of pure bread,
    Whose appetites are dead:
    No, give them grains their fill,
    Husks, draff to drink, and swill:
If they love lees, and leave the lusty wine,
Envy them not, their palate's with the swine.   20

No doubt a mouldy tale,
    Like Pericles, and stale
As the shrieve's crust, and nasty as his fish,
    Scraps out of every dish,
Thrown forth and raked into the common tub,
    May keep up the play club.
    Broome's sweepings do as well
    There, as his master's meal:
For who the relish of these guests will fit,
Needs set them but the alms-basket of wit.   30

And much good do it ye then,
    Brave plush and velvet men
Can feed on orts; and safe in your scene clothes,
    Dare quit upon your oaths
The stagers, and the stage-wrights too; your peers,
    Of stuffing your large ears
    With rage of comic socks,
    Wrought upon twenty blocks;
Which, if they're torn, and foul, and patched enough,
40 The gamesters share your gilt, and you their stuff.

    Leave things so prostitute,
    And take the Alcaic lute;
Or thine own Horace, or Anacreon's lyre;
    Warm thee by Pindar's fire:
And though thy nerves be shrunk, and blood be cold,
    Ere years have made thee old,
    Strike that disdainful heat
    Throughout, to their defeat:
As curious fools, and envious of thy strain,
50 May blushing swear, no palsy's in thy brain.

    But when they hear thee sing
    The glories of thy king;
His zeal to God, and his just awe of men,
    They may be blood-shaken, then
Feel such a flesh-quake to possess their powers,
    That no tuned harp like ours,
    In sound of peace or wars,
    Shall truly hit the stars
When they shall read the acts of Charles his reign,
60 And see his chariot triumph 'bove his wain.

A Song of the Moon

∽

To the wonders of the Peak,
I am come to add, and speak,
Or as some would say to break
   My mind unto you,
And I swear by all the light
At my back, I am no sprite,
But a very merry wight
   Pressed in to see you.

I had somewhat else to say,
But have lost it by the way,   10
I shall think on't ere't be day.
   The moon commends her
To the merry beards in hall,
Those turned up, and those that fall,
Morts, and mirkins that wag all,
   Tough, foul, or tender.

And as either news of mirth
Rise or fall upon the earth
She desires of every birth
   Some taste to send her.   20
Specially the news of Derby;
For if there or peace or war be,
To the Peak it is so hard by,
   She soon will hear it.

If there be a cuckold major,
That the wife heads for a wager
As the standard shall engage her,
   The moon will bear it.
Though she change as oft as she,
And of circle be as free,   30
Or her quarters lighter be,
   Yet do not fear it.

Or if any strife betide
For the breeches with the bride,
'Tis but the next neighbour ride
   And she is pleased.
Or if it be the gossips' hap
Each to pawn her husband's cap,
At Pem Waker's good ale tap,
40   Her mind is eased.

Or by chance if in their grease
Or their ale, they break the peace,
Forfeiting their drinking lease,
   She will not seize it.

A Panegyre, on the Happy Entrance of James, Our Sovereign, to His First High Session of Parliament in This Kingdom, the 19 of March, 1603

∽

Heaven now not strives, alone, our breasts to fill
With joys: but urgeth his full favours still.
Again, the glory of our western world
Unfolds himself: and from his eyes are hurled
(Today) a thousand radiant lights, that stream
To every nook and angle of his realm.
His former rays did only clear the sky;
But these his searching beams are cast, to pry
Into those dark and deep concealèd vaults,
10 Where men commit black incest with their faults;
And snore supinely in the stall of sin,
Where murder, rapine, lust, do sit within,
Carousing human blood in iron bowls,

And make their den the slaughter-house of souls:
From whose foul reeking caverns first arise
Those damps, that so offend all good men's eyes;
And would (if not dispersed) infect the crown,
And in their vapour her bright metal drown.
   To this so clear and sanctified an end,
I saw, when reverend Themis did descend   20
Upon his state; let down in that rich chain,
That fasteneth heavenly power to earthly reign:
Beside her, stooped on either hand, a maid,
Fair Dice, and Eunomia; who were said
To be her daughters: and but faintly known
On earth, till now they came to grace his throne.
Her third, Irene, helped to bear his train;
And in her office vowed she would remain,
Till foreign malice, or unnatural spite
(Which Fates avert) should force her from her right.   30
With these he passed, and with his people's hearts
Breathed in his way; and souls (their better parts)
Hasting to follow forth in shouts, and cries;
Upon his face all threw their covetous eyes,
As on a wonder: some amazèd stood,
As if they felt, but had not known their good:
Others would fain have shown it in their words:
But, when their speech so poor a help affords
Unto their zeal's expression; they are mute:
And only with red silence him salute.   40
Some cry from tops of houses; thinking noise
The fittest herald to proclaim true joys:
Others on ground run gazing by his side,
All, as unwearied, as unsatisfied:
And every window grieved it could not move
Along with him, and the same trouble prove.
They that had seen, but four short days before,
His gladding look, now longed to see it more.
And as of late, when he through London went,
The amorous city spared no ornament,   50
That might her beauties heighten; but so dressed,

As our ambitious dames, when they make feast,
And would be courted: so this town put on
Her brightest tire; and, in it, equal shone
To her great sister; save that modesty,
Her place, and years, gave her precedency.
  The joy of either was alike, and full;
No age, nor sex, so weak, or strongly dull,
That did not bear a part in this consent
60 Of hearts and voices. All the air was rent,
As with the murmur of a moving wood;
The ground beneath did seem a moving flood:
Walls, windows, roofs, towers, steeples, all were set
With several eyes, that in this object met.
Old men were glad, their fates till now did last;
And infants, that the hours had made such haste
To bring them forth; whilst riper aged, and apt
To understand the more, the more were rapt.
This was the people's love, with which did strive
70 The nobles' zeal, yet either kept alive
The other's flame, as doth the wick and wax,
That friendly tempered, one pure taper makes.
Meanwhile, the reverend Themis draws aside
The king's obeying will, from taking pride
In these vain stirs, and to his mind suggests
How he may triumph in his subjects' breasts,
With better pomp. She tells him first, that kings
Are here on earth the most conspicuous things:
That they, by Heaven, are placed upon his throne,
80 To rule like Heaven; and have no more, their own,
As they are men, than men. That all they do
Though hid at home, abroad is searched into:
And, being once found out, discovered lies
Unto as many envies, there, as eyes.
That princes, since they know it is their fate,
Oft-times, to have the secrets of their state
Betrayed to fame, should take more care, and fear
In public acts what form and face they bear.
She then remembered to his thought the place

Where he was going; and the upward race   90
Of kings, preceding him in that high court;
Their laws, their ends; the men she did report:
And all so justly, as his ear was joyed
To hear the truth, from spite, or flattery void.
She showed him, who made wise, who honest acts;
Who both, who neither: all the cunning tracts,
And thriving statutes she could promptly note;
The bloody, base, and barbarous she did quote;
Where laws were made to serve the tyrant will;
Where sleeping they could save, and waking kill;   100
Where acts gave licence to impetuous lust
To bury churches, in forgotten dust,
And with their ruins raise the pandar's bowers:
When, public justice borrowed all her powers
From private chambers; that could then create
Laws, judges, councillors, yea prince, and state.
All this she told, and more, with bleeding eyes;
For Right is as compassionate as wise.
Nor did he seem their vices so to love,
As once defend, what Themis did reprove.   110
For though by right, and benefit of times,
He owned their crowns, he would not so their crimes.
He knew that princes, who had sold their fame
To their voluptuous lusts, had lost their name;
And that no wretch was more unblessed than he,
Whose necessary good 'twas now to be
An evil king: and so must such be still,
Who once have got the habit to do ill.
One wickedness another must defend;
For vice is safe, while she hath vice to friend.   120
He knew, that those, who would, with love, command,
Must with a tender (yet a steadfast) hand
Sustain the reins, and in the check forbear
To offer cause of injury, or fear.
That kings, by their example, more do sway
Than by their power; and men do more obey
When they are led than when they are compelled.

In all these knowing arts our prince excelled.
And now the dame had dried her dropping eyne,
130 When, like an April Iris, flew her shine
About the streets, as it would force a spring
From out the stones, to gratulate the king.
She blessed the people, that in shoals did swim
To hear her speech; which still began in him
And ceased in them. She told them, what a fate
Was gently fallen from heaven upon this state;
How dear a father they did now enjoy
That came to save, what discord would destroy:
And entering with the power of a king,
140 The temperance of a private man did bring,
That won affections, ere his steps won ground;
And was not hot, or covetous to be crowned
Before men's hearts had crowned him. Who (unlike
Those greater bodies of the sky, that strike
The lesser fires dim) in his access
Brighter than all, hath yet made no one less;
Though many greater: and the most, the best.
Wherein his choice was happy with the rest
Of his great actions, first to see, and do
150 What all men's wishes did aspire unto.
    Hereat, the people could no longer hold
Their bursting joys; but through the air was rolled
The lengthened shout, as when the artillery
Of heaven is discharged along the sky:
And this confession flew from every voice:
'Never had land more reason to rejoice.
Nor to her bliss, could aught now added be,
Save, that she might the same perpetual see.'
Which when Time, Nature, and the Fates denied,
160 With a twice louder shout again they cried,
'Yet, let blessèd Britain ask (without your wrong)
Still to have such a king, and this king long.'

Solus Rex, et Poeta non quotannis nascitur.

Over the Door at the Entrance into the Apollo

∞

Welcome all that lead or follow,
To the oracle of Apollo –
Here he speaks out of his pottle,
Or the tripos, his tower bottle:
All his answers are divine,
Truth itself doth flow in wine.
Hang up all the poor hop-drinkers,
Cries old Sym, the king of skinkers;
He the half of life abuses,
That sits watering with the muses.   10
Those dull girls no good can mean us,
Wine, it is the milk of Venus,
And the poet's horse accounted:
Ply it, and you all are mounted.
'Tis the true Phoebian liquor,
Cheers the brains, makes wit the quicker,
Pays all debts, cures all diseases,
And at once three senses pleases.
Welcome, all that lead or follow,
To the oracle of Apollo.   20

159

An Expostulation with Inigo Jones

Master Surveyor, you that first began
From thirty pound in pipkins, to the man
You are; from them leapt forth an architect,
Able to talk of Euclid, and correct
Both him and Archimede; damn Architas,
The noblest engineer that ever was!
Control Ctesibius: overbearing us
With mistook names out of Vitruvius!
Drawn Aristotle on us! And thence shown
10 How much architectonic is your own!
Whether the building of the stage or scene,
Or making of the properties it mean!
Visors or antics! Or it comprehend
Something your sir-ship doth not yet intend!
By all your titles, and whole style at once
Of tire-man, mountebank and Justice Jones,
I do salute you! Are you fitted yet?
Will any of these express your place or wit?
Or are you so ambitious 'bove your peers
20 You would be an asinigo, by your ears?
Why, much good do it you! Be what beast you will,
You'll be, as Langley said, an Inigo still.
   What makes your wretchedness to bray so loud
In town and court? Are you grown rich and proud?
Your trapping will not change you. Change your mind:
No velvet sheath you wear, will alter kind.
A wooden dagger, is a dagger of wood
Though gold or ivory hafts would make it good.
What is the cause you pomp it so? I ask,
30 And all men echo, you have made a masque.
I chime that too: and I have met with those
That do cry up the machine, and the shows!
The majesty of Juno in the clouds,

And peering forth of Iris in the shrouds!
The ascent of Lady Fame which none could spy;
Not they that sided her, Dame Poetry,
Dame History, Dame Architecture too,
And Goody Sculpture, brought with much ado
To hold her up. O shows, shows, mighty shows!
The eloquence of masques! What need of prose,   40
Or verse, or sense to express immortal you?
You are the spectacles of state! 'Tis true
Court hieroglyphics, and all arts afford
In the mere perspective of an inch board!
You ask no more than certain politic eyes,
Eyes that can pierce into the mysteries
Of many colours, read them, and reveal
Mythology there painted on slit deal!
O, to make boards to speak! There is a task!
Painting and carpentry are the soul of masque!   50
Pack with your peddling poetry to the stage,
This is the money-get, mechanic age!
To plant the music where no ear can reach,
Attire the persons as no thought can teach
Sense what they are, which by a specious fine
Term of the architects is called design!
But in the practised truth destruction is
Of any art, beside what he calls his!
Whither, O whither will this tireman grow?
His name is *Skeuopoios* we all know,   60
The maker of the properties; in sum
The scene, the engine! But he now is come
To be the music master, fabler too!
He is, or would be, the main dominus-do-
All in the work! And so shall still for Ben:
Be Inigo, the whistle, and his men!
He's warm on his feet now, he says, and can
Swim without cork! Why, thank the good Queen Anne.
I am too fat to envy him. He too lean
To be worth envy. Henceforth I do mean   70
To pity him, as smiling at his feat

Of lantern-lerry: with fuliginous heat
Whirling his whimsies, by a subtlety
Sucked from the veins of shop-philosophy.
What would he do now, giving his mind that way
In presentation of some puppet play!
Should but the king his justicehood employ
In setting forth of such a solemn toy!
How would he firk like Adam Overdo
80 Up and about! Dive into cellars too,
Disguised, and thence drag forth enormity,
Discover vice, commit absurdity,
Under the moral! Show he had a pate
Moulded or stroked up to survey a state!
O wise surveyor, wiser architect,
But wisest Inigo! Who can reflect
On the new priming of thy old sign posts
Reviving with fresh colours the pale ghosts
Of thy dead standards: or (with miracle) see
90 Thy twice conceived, thrice paid for imagery?
And not fall down before it and confess
Almighty architecture? Who no less
A goddess is, than painted cloth, deal boards,
Vermilion, lake, or cinnopar affords
Expression for, with that unbounded line
Aimed at in thy omnipotent design!
What poesy e'er was painted on a wall
That might compare with thee? What story shall
Of all the Worthies hope to outlast thy one,
100 So the materials be of Purbeck stone?
Live long the Feasting Room. And ere thou burn
Again, thy architect to ashes turn!
Whom not ten fires, nor a parliament can
With all remonstrance make an honest man.

∽

Slow, slow, fresh fount, keep time with my salt tears;
   Yet, slower, yet; O faintly, gentle springs:
List to the heavy part the music bears,
   Woe weeps out her division, when she sings.
      Droop herbs, and flowers,
      Fall grief in showers,
      Our beauties are not ours:
        O, I could still,
Like melting snow upon some craggy hill,
     Drop, drop, drop, drop,   10
Since nature's pride is, now, a withered daffodil.

∽

   Queen and huntress, chaste, and fair,
   Now the sun is laid to sleep,
   Seated, in thy silver chair,
   State in wonted manner keep:
      Hesperus entreats thy light,
      Goddess, excellently bright.

   Earth, let not thy envious shade
   Dare itself to interpose;
   Cynthia's shining orb was made
   Heaven to clear, when day did close: 10
      Bless us then with wishèd sight,
      Goddess, excellently bright.

   Lay thy bow of pearl apart,
   And thy crystal-shining quiver;

Give unto the flying hart
Space to breathe, how short soever:
    Thou, that mak'st a day of night,
    Goddess, excellently bright.

∽

Fools, they are the only nation
Worth men's envy, or admiration;
Free from care, or sorrow-taking,
Selves, and others merry making:
All they speak, or do, is sterling.
Your fool, he is your great man's darling,
And your lady's sport and pleasure;
Tongue and bauble are his treasure.
E'en his face begetteth laughter,
10 And he speaks truth free from slaughter;
He's the grace of every feast,
And, sometimes, the chiefest guest;
Hath his trencher, and his stool,
When wit waits upon the fool.
    O, who would not be
    He, he, he?

∽

Still to be neat, still to be dressed,
As you were going to a feast;
Still to be powdered, still perfumed:
Lady, it is to be presumed,
Though art's hid causes are not found,

All is not sweet, all is not sound.
Give me a look, give me a face,
That makes simplicity a grace;
Robes loosely flowing, hair as free:
Such sweet neglect more taketh me,   10
Than all the adulteries of art;
They strike mine eyes, but not my heart.

∽

My masters and friends, and good people draw near,
And look to your purses, for that I do say;
And though little money, in them you do bear,
It cost more to get, than to lose in a day.
      You oft have been told,
      Both the young and the old;
      And bidden beware of the cutpurse so bold;
Then if you take heed not, free me from the curse,
Who both give you warning for, and the cutpurse.
Youth, youth, thou hadst better been starved by thy nurse   10
Than live to be hanged for cutting a purse.

It hath been upbraided to men of my trade,
That oftentimes we are the cause of this crime.
Alack and for pity, why should it be said?
As if they regarded or places, or time.
      Examples have been
      Of some that were seen,
      In Westminster Hall, yea the pleaders
      between:
Then why should the judges be free from this curse,
More than my poor self, for cutting the purse?   20
Youth, youth, thou hadst better been starved by thy nurse,
Than live to be hanged for cutting a purse.

At Worcester 'tis known well, and even i' the gaol,
A knight of good worship did there show his face,
Against the foul sinners, in zeal for to rail.
And lost (*ipso facto*) his purse in the place.
   Nay, once from the seat
   Of judgment so great,
   A judge there did lose a fair pouch of velvet.

30 O Lord for thy mercy, how wicked or worse,
Are those that so venture their necks for a purse!
Youth, youth, thou hadst better be starved by thy nurse,
Than live to be hanged for cutting a purse.

At plays and at sermons, and at the sessions,
'Tis daily their practice such booty to make:
Yea, under the gallows, at executions,
They stick not the stareabouts' purses to take.
   Nay one without grace,
   At a far better place,
40   At court and in Christmas, before the King's
    face.
Alack then for pity, must I bear the curse,
That only belongs to the cunning cutpurse?

But O, you vile nation of cutpurses all,
Relent and repent, and amend and be sound,
And know that you ought not, by honest men's fall,
Advance your own fortunes, to die above ground,
   And though you go gay,
   In silks as you may,
   It is not the high way to heaven (as they say)
50 Repent then, repent you, for better, for worse:
And kiss not the gallows for cutting a purse.
Youth, youth, thou hadst better been starved by thy nurse,
Than live to be hanged for cutting a purse.

∽

It was a beauty that I saw,
So pure, so perfect, as the frame
Of all the universe was lame,
To that one figure, could I draw,
Or give least line of it a law!

A skein of silk without a knot,
A fair march made without a halt,
A curious form without a fault,
A printed book without a blot,
All beauty, and without a spot!   10

SONGS FROM JONSON'S MASQUES
AND ENTERTAINMENTS

Epithalamion

∽

Up, youths and virgins, up, and praise
The god whose nights outshine his days;
 Hymen, whose hallowed rites
Could never boast of brighter lights;
 Whose bands pass liberty.
Two of your troop, that with the morn were free,
 Are now waged to his war.
  And what they are,
 If you'll perfection see,
  Yourselves must be.   10
Shine, Hesperus, shine forth, thou wishèd star!

What joy or honours can compare
With holy nuptials, when they are
   Made out of equal parts
Of years, of states, of hands, of hearts!
   When in the happy choice
The spouse and spousèd have the foremost voice!
     Such, glad of Hymen's war,
       Live what they are,
20   And long perfection see:
       And such ours be.
Shine, Hesperus, shine forth, thou wishèd star!

The solemn state of this one night
Were fit to last an age's light;
   But there are rites behind
Have less of state, but more of kind:
   Love's wealthy crop of kisses,
And fruitful harvest of his mother's blisses.
     Sound then to Hymen's war:
30   That what these are,
     Who will perfection see,
       May haste to be.
Shine, Hesperus, shine forth, thou wishèd star!

Love's commonwealth consists of toys;
His council are those antic boys,
   Games, laughter, sports, delights,
That triumph with him on these nights;
   To whom we must give way,
For now their reign begins, and lasts till day.
40   They sweeten Hymen's war,
       And in that jar,
     Make all that married be
       Perfection see.
Shine, Hesperus, shine forth, thou wishèd star!

Why stays the bridegroom to invade
Her that would be a matron made?
 Goodnight whilst yet we may
Goodnight to you a virgin say:
 Tomorrow rise the same
Your mother is, and use a nobler name.   50
  Speed well in Hymen's war,
   That, what you are,
  By your perfection we
   And all may see.
Shine, Hesperus, shine forth, thou wishèd star!

Tonight is Venus' vigil kept,
This night no bridegroom ever slept;
 And if the fair bride do,
The married say, 'tis his fault too.
  Wake then, and let your lights   60
Wake too; for they'll tell nothing of your nights,
  But that in Hymen's war
   You perfect are.
  And such perfection we
   Do pray should be.
Shine, Hesperus, shine forth, thou wishèd star!

That ere the rosy-fingered morn
Behold nine moons, there may be born
 A babe, to uphold the fame
Of Ratcliffe's blood and Ramsey's name: 70
  That may, in his great seed,
Wear the long honours of his father's deed.
  Such fruits of Hymen's war
   Most perfect are;
  And all perfection we
   Wish you should see.
Shine, Hesperus, shine forth, thou wishèd star!

Charm

∞

The owl is abroad, the bat, and the toad,
    And so is the cat-a-mountain,
The ant, and the mole fit both in a hole,
    The frog peeps out of the fountain;
The dogs, they do bay, and the timbrels play,
    The spindle is now a-turning;
The moon it is red, and the stars are fled,
    But all the sky is a-burning:
The ditch is made, and our nails the spade,
10 With pictures full, of wax, and of wool;
Their livers I stick, with needles quick;
There lacks but the blood, to make up the flood.
    Quickly, dame, then bring your part in,
Spur, spur, upon little Martin,
Merrily, merrily, make him sail,
A worm in his mouth, and a thorn in his tail,
Fire above, and fire below,
With a whip in your hand, to make him go.
      O, now she's come!
20   Let all be dumb.

∞

Buzz, quoth the blue-fly,
  Hum, quoth the bee;
Buzz and hum they cry,
  And so do we.
In his ear, in his nose,
  Thus, do you see?
  He ate the dormouse,
    Else it was he.

∞

Now, my cunning lady moon,
Can you leave the side so soon
  Of the boy you keep so hid?
Midwife Juno sure will say
This is not the proper way
  Of your paleness to be rid.
But perhaps it is your grace
To wear sickness in your face,
  That there might be wagers laid
  Still, by fools, you are a maid.   10

Come, your changes overthrow
What your look would carry so;
  Moon, confess then what you are.
And be wise, and free to use
Pleasures that you now do lose:
  Let us satyrs have a share.
Though our forms be rough and rude,
Yet our acts may be endued
  With more virtue: everyone
  Cannot be Endymion.   20

∞

What just excuse had agèd Time,
    His weary limbs now to have eased,
And sat him down without his crime,
    While every thought was so much pleased!
For he so greedy to devour
    His own, and all that he brings forth,
Is eating every piece of hour
    Some object of the rarest worth.
Yet this is rescued from his rage,
10   As not to die by time or age.
    For beauty hath a living name
    And will to heaven, from whence it came.

∞

O how came Love, that is himself a fire,
    To be so cold!
Yes, tyran' money quencheth all desire,
    Or makes it old.
But here are beauties will revive
Love's youth and keep his heat alive:
    As often as his torch here dies,
    He needs but light it at fresh eyes.
Joy, joy the more; for in all courts
10   If Love be cold, so are his sports.

∽

Soft, subtle fire, thou soul of art,
 Now do thy part
On weaker nature, that through age is lamed.
  Take but thy time, now she is old,
  And the sun her friend grown cold,
She will no more, in strife with thee be named.

Look, but how few confess her now,
 In cheek or brow!
From every head, almost, how she is frighted!
  That very age abhors her so,   10
  That it learns to speak and go
As if by art alone it could be righted.

∽

Hum drum, sauce for a cony;
 No more of your martial music;
Even for the sake of the next new stake,
 For there I do mean to use it.

And now to ye, who in place are to see,
 With roll and farthingale hoopèd:
I pray you know, though he want his bow,
 By the wings that this is Cupid.

He might go back, for to cry 'What you lack?'
 But that were not so witty: 10
His cap and coat are enough to note,
 That he is the Love of the city.

And he leads on, though he now be gone,
 For that was only his rule:

But now comes in Tom of Bosom's Inn,
   And he presenteth misrule.

Which you may know by the very show,
   Albeit you never ask it:
For there you may see what his ensigns be,
20   The rope, the cheese, and the basket.

This carol plays, and has been in his days
   A chirping boy and a kill-pot;
Kit-cobbler it is, I'm a father of his,
   And he dwells in the lane called Fill-pot.

But who is this? O, my daughter Cis
   Mince-pie; with her do not dally
On pain of your life: she's an honest cook's wife,
   And comes out of Scalding Alley.

Next in the trace comes Gambol in place;
30   And to make my tale the shorter,
My son Hercules, ta'en out of Distaff Lane,
   But an active man and a porter.

Now Post and Pair, old Christmas' heir,
   Doth make and a jingling sally;
And wot you who, 'tis one of my two
   Sons, card-makers in Pur Alley.

Next in a trice, with his box and his dice,
   MacPippin my son, but younger,
Brings Mumming in; and the knave will win,
40   For he is a costermonger.

But New Year's Gift of himself makes shift
   To tell you what his name is:
With orange on head and his gingerbread,
   Clem Wasp of Honey Lane 'tis.

This I tell you is our jolly wassail,
   And for Twelfth Night more meet, too:
She works by the ell, and her name is Nell,
   And she dwells in Threadneedle Street, too.

Then Offering, he, with his dish and his tree,
    That in every great house keepeth,   50
Is by my son, young Littleworth, done,
    And in Penny-rich Street he sleepeth.

Last, Baby-cake, that an end doth make
    Of Christmas' merry, merry vein-a,
Is Child Rowlan, and a straight young man,
    Though he come out of Crooked Lane-a.

There should have been, and a dozen I ween,
    But I could find but one more
Child of Christmas, and a log it was,
    When I them all had gone o'er.   60

I prayed him, in a time so trim,
    That he would make one to prance it:
And I myself would have been the twelfth,
    O, but Log was too heavy to dance it.

∽

Break, Fant'sy, from thy cave of cloud
    And spread thy purple wings;
Now all thy figures are allowed,
    And various shapes of things;
Create of airy forms a stream;
    It must have blood and nought of phlegm,
And though it be a waking dream,
        Yet let it like an odour rise
        To all the senses here,
        And fall like sleep upon their eyes,   10
        Or music in their ear.

Hymn

∞

Room, room, make room for the bouncing belly,
First father of sauce, and deviser of jelly,
Prime master of arts, and the giver of wit,
That found out the excellent engine, the spit,
The plough, and the flail, the mill, and the hopper,
The hutch, and the boulter, the furnace, and copper,
The oven, the bavin, the mawkin, the peel,
The hearth, and the range, the dog and the wheel,
He, he first invented the hogshead and tun,
10 The gimlet and vice too, and taught 'em to run.
And since, with the funnel, an Hippocras bag
He's made of himself, that now he cries swag.
Which shows, though the pleasure be but of four
   inches,
Yet he is a weasel, the gullet that pinches,
Of any delight, and not spares from the back
Whatever to make of the belly a sack.
Hail, hail, plump paunch, O the founder of taste
For fresh meats, or powdered, or pickle, or paste;
Devourer of broiled, baked, roasted or sod,
20 And emptier of cups, be they even or odd;
All which have now made thee so wide in the waist
As scarce with no pudding thou art to be laced;
But eating and drinking until thou dost nod,
Thou break'st all thy girdles, and break'st forth a god.

∽

From the famous Peak of Derby,
And the Devil's Arse there hard by,
Where we yearly keep our musters,
Thus the Egyptians throng in clusters.

Be not frighted with our fashion,
Though we seem a tattered nation;
We account our rags our riches,
So our tricks exceed our stitches.

Give us bacon, rinds of walnuts,
Shells of cockles, and of small nuts,   10
Ribands, bells, and saffroned linen,
All the world is ours to win in.

Knacks we have that will delight you,
Slights of hand that will invite you
To endure our tawny faces,
And not cause you cut your laces.

All your fortunes we can tell ye,
Be they for the back or belly:
In the moods too, and the tenses,
That may fit your fine five senses.   20

Draw but then your gloves, we pray you,
And sit still, we will not fray you;
For though we be here at Burleigh,
We'd be loth to make a hurly.

∽

The fairy beam upon you,
The stars to glister on you:
    A moon of light,
    In the noon of night,
Till the fire-drake hath o'er-gone you.

The wheel of fortune guide you,
The boy with the bow beside you
    Run aye in the way,
    Till the bird of day,
10   And the luckier lot betide you.

∽

Cocklorrel woulds needs have the devil his guest,
    And bade him once into the Peak to dinner,
Where never the fiend had such a feast
    Provided him yet at the charge of a sinner.

His stomach was queasy (he came hither coached)
    The jogging had caused some crudities rise;
To help it he called for a puritan poached,
    That used to turn up the eggs of his eyes.

And so recovered unto his wish,
10   He sat him down, and he fell to eat;
Promoter in plum broth was the first dish –
    His own privy kitchen had no such meat.

Yet though with this he much were taken,
    Upon a sudden he shifted his trencher,
As soon as he spied the bawd and the bacon,
    By which you may note the devil's a wencher.

Six pickled tailors sliced and cut,
    Sempsters and tirewomen, fit for his palate;
With feathermen and perfumers put
    Some twelve in a charger to make a great sallet.   20

A rich fat usurer stewed in his marrow,
    And by him a lawyer's head and green sauce:
Both which his belly took up like a barrow,
    As if till then he had never seen sauce.

Then carbonadoed and cooked with pains,
    Was brought up a cloven sergeant's face:
The sauce was made of his yeoman's brains,
    That had been beaten out with his own mace.

Two roasted sherriffs came whole to the board;
    (The feast had been nothing without 'em)   30
Both living and dead they were foxed and furred,
    Their chains like sausages hung about 'em.

The very next dish was the mayor of a town,
    With a pudding of maintenance thrust in his belly,
Like a goose in the feathers, dressed in his gown,
    And his couple of hinch-boys boiled to a jelly.

A London cuckold hot from the spit,
    And when the carver up had broken him,
The devil chopped up his head at a bit,
    But the horns were very near like to choke him.   40

The chine of a lecher too there was roasted,
    With a plump harlot's haunch and garlic,
A pandar's pettitoes, that had boasted
    Himself for a captain, yet never was warlike.

A large fat pasty of a midwife hot;
    And for a cold baked meat into the story,
A reverend painted lady was brought,
    And coffined in crust till now she was hoary.

To these, an over-grown justice of peace,
50   With a clerk like a gizzard trussed under each arm;
And warrants for sippits, laid in his own grease,
     Set over a chafing dish to be kept warm.

The jowl of a gaoler served for fish,
     A constable soused with vinegar by;
Two aldermen lobsters asleep in a dish.
     A deputy tart, a churchwarden pie.

All which devoured, he then for a close
     Did for a full draught of Derby call;
He heaved the huge vessel up to his nose,
60   And left not till he had drunk up all.

Then from the table he gave a start,
     Where banquet and wine were nothing scarce,
All which he flirted away with a fart,
     From whence it was called the Devil's Arse.

Ballad

∞

Though it may seem rude
For me to intrude,
     With these my bears, by chance-a;
'Twere sport for a king,
If they could sing
     As well as they can dance-a.

Then to put you out
Of fear or doubt,
     We came from St Katherine-a;

These dancing three,   10
By the help of me,
    Who am the post of the sign-a.
We sell good ware,
And we need not care
    Though court and country knew it;
Our ale's of the best,
And each good guest
    Prays for the soul that brew it.

For any ale-house,
We care not a louse,   20
    Nor tavern in all the town-a;
Nor the Vintry Cranes,
Nor St Clement Danes,
    Nor the Devil can put us down-a.

Who has once there been,
Comes hither again,
    The liquor is so mighty;
Beer strong and stale,
And so is our ale,
    And it burns like aqua-vitae.   30

To a stranger there,
If any appear,
    Where never before he has been:
We show the iron gate,
The wheel of St Kate,
    And the place where the priest fell in.

The wives of Wapping,
They trudge to our tapping,
    And there our ale desire:
And they sit and drink,   40
Till they spew and stink,
    And often piss out our fire.

From morning to night,
And about to daylight,
    They sit, and never grudge it;
Till the fishwives join
Their single coin,
    And the tinker pawns his budget.

If their brains be not well,
50 Or their bladders do swell,
    To ease them of their burden,
My lady will come
With a bowl and a broom,
    And her handmaid with a jordan.

From court we invite
Lord, lady, and knight,
    Squire, gentleman, yeoman, and groom;
And all our stiff drinkers,
Smiths, porters, and tinkers,
60   And the beggars shall give ye room.

NOTES

EPIGRAMS

Epigrams I was published as part of the 1616 folio *Works* and dedicated to William Herbert, third Earl of Pembroke (1580–1630). Jonson called his epigrams 'the ripest of my studies', and they represent the most serious attempt up to 1616 to reproduce in English the epigrams of Martial. The collection can be seen as a single work, in which satire and praise conduct a dialogue which enacts in miniature the tension that runs through Jonson's work, between his sensitivity to corruption and his belief in human virtue.

To My Bookseller

Originally intended for John Stepneth, the bookseller, in 1612.
8   *cleft sticks*   this seems to refer to sticks used to hold open pages of a book to show off its title page.
9   *termers*   visitors to London during term-time at the Inns of Court.

To King James

2–5   James's *His Maiesties Poeticall Exercises* was published in 1591 and his *Essays of a Prentise* in 1584.

On the Union

Title   The union is that between England and Scotland. James spoke of the idea of a single nation in his first speech to the English parliament. The poem was written in 1604.

On the New Hot-House

Title   *Hot-House*   the poem is built on the double meaning of this word: 'brothel' and 'bath-house'.

On a Robbery

1 *Ridway ... Duncote* these names have not been identified and may be fictional.

On Lieutenant Shift

Title there is a character of this name in *Every Man out of His Humour*.
11 *ordinaries* gambling houses.
16 *the papers* in which drugs were wrapped.
21 *cockatrice* whore.

To Doctor Empiric

2 *Aesculape* Aesculapius, the god of medicine, was the son of Apollo and Coronis.

To William Camden

Title William Camden (1551–1623) was Jonson's master at Westminster and the author of *Britannia* (1586).

To the Learnèd Critic

6 *the chaste tree* the laurel, into which Daphne was transformed to save her from rape by Apollo.

To My Mere English Censurer

Title *Mere* wholly, absolutely (in the sense of someone whose horizons are completely parochial; specifically here someone who knows nothing about the nature of the classical epigram).
4 Sir John Davies's *Epigrams* were printed *c.* 1590, and John Weever's *Epigrams in the Oldest Cut* in 1599.

On Reformed Gamester

4 *the Word* the Bible.
6 *bastinado* a stick used for beating the victim, usually on the soles of the feet (so there may be a pun – soul/sole – in l. 8).

On My First Daughter

Title This child may have been called Mary, and it seems probable that she was born and died in 1601.

To John Donne

1 *Phoebus* Apollo, god of poetry.
2 *refuse* the syntax leading up to this verb is ambiguous, but the meaning seems to be 'Phoebus and each of the muses reject all brains in favour of yours'.

On Sir Voluptuous Beast

4 *Ganymede* a Trojan prince who became cupbearer to Zeus. Here, as commonly at this time, 'homosexual partner'.
5 *cucqueen* female cuckold.
8 *make woman's haste* i.e., behave in a sexually untrustworthy way (as, conventionally, women were inclined – so males thought – to do).

On Sir John Roe ('In place of scutcheons . . .')

Title *Sir John Roe* born 1581, son of a merchant tailor; travelled to Moscow; served in Ireland; minor poet; died ?1606 of the plague.

On Don Surly

Title *Surly* also a character in *The Alchemist*.
4 *rhinocerote's nose* sneeringly.
7 *tympanies* tumours.

To Sir Annual Tilter

3 *device* a pictorial representation of an object or objects with a verbal motto, usually expressive of a person's principles or aspirations.

On Sir John Roe ('What two brave perils . . .')

Title See note above for *On Sir John Roe* ('*In place of scutcheons* . . .'). Presumably written around 1606.
3 *self-divided Belgia* the Pacification of Ghent (1576) had united

Holland and Belgium, but in 1579 Calvinist–Catholic tension again divided the Netherlands.

10   *serenes*   cool evening dampnesses.

To the Same

Presumably also written around 1606. See *On Sir John Roe* ('*What two brave perils . . .*').

To King James

This poem was probably written in 1604.

To Robert, Earl of Salisbury ('What need hast thou of me . . .')

This poem was written in 1605. Robert Cecil (?1563–1605) was made Secretary of State in 1596 and created Earl of Salisbury in 1605.

On My First Son

This poem was written in 1603, the year of the child's death.

1   *child of my right hand*   the boy's name was Benjamin, which in Hebrew means 'fortunate' or 'dexterous'. The latter basically means 'right-handed', with the additional English sense of 'essential', so there is a kind of trilingual pun here.

To Francis Beaumont

Beaumont (*c.* 1584–1616) was the son of Francis Beaumont, a Justice of Common Pleas. He was educated at Oxford and the Inner Temple, and became a poet and playwright.

On Poet-Ape

3   *brocage*   dealing in castoffs.

To Fine Lady Would-Be

Lady Would-Be is also a character in *Volpone* (1606).

To Robert, Earl of Salisbury ('Who can consider . . .')

Title See note above to *Robert, Earl of Salisbury* ('*What need hast thou . . .*').

To Thomas, Earl of Suffolk

Title Thomas Howard (1561–1626); Earl of Suffolk (1603); Lord Chamberlain (1603–14); Lord High Treasurer (1614–19).

To Thomas, Lord Chancellor

Title *Thomas, Lord Chancellor* Thomas Egerton (?1540–1617) was Solicitor General (1581), Attorney General (1592), Master of the Rolls (1594), Lord Keeper (1596) and Lord Chancellor (1603).

On Lucy, Countess of Bedford

Title She was the daughter of John, first Baron Harington, and married Edward, third Earl of Bedford, in 1594. She was patron to such as Jonson, Donne, Daniel and Drayton, and died in 1627.
15 *The rock . . . shears* emblems of the Fates: Clotho spun the thread of life (rock = distaff); Lachesis decided its length; Atropos cut the thread to end the life.

To Edward Alleyn

Alleyn (1566–1626) was an actor and theatre impresario who founded Dulwich College in 1619.
3 *Roscius . . . Aesop* classical epitomes of, respectively, comic and tragic actors.

On Mill, My Lady's Woman

4 *wan* won.
17 *Milo* Milo of Crotona was a famous Greek athlete of the sixth century BC.
  wull will.

To Sir Horace Vere

Vere (1565–1635) was a soldier who fought with distinction in the Netherlands, being made Baron Vere of Tilbury for his relief of the siege of Breda in 1625.

1–3 Jonson links Vere's surname with Latin 'vere' (truly) and his Christian name with the Roman poet Horace.

To Sir Thomas Roe

Roe (1581–1644) was knighted in 1605, ambassador to the Great Mogul (1614) and Chancellor of the Garter (1621).

Inviting a Friend to Supper

8 *cates* food, provisions.
9 *rectify* remove impurities from (a chemical term).
19 *godwit* a marsh bird rather like a curlew.
20 *Knat* a bird of the snipe family.
 rail a bird of the family Rallidae.
 ruff a male bird of the sandpiper family.
36 *Pooly ... Parrot* Robert Pooly betrayed Babington in 1586; Parrot is unidentified.

To Mary, Lady Wroth ('How well, fair crown ...')

Title Mary was the eldest daughter of Robert Dudley, first Earl of Leicester, and niece of Sir Philip Sidney. She married Sir Robert Wroth in 1604.
7 *imprese* badge, device.

To Mary, Lady Wroth ('Madam, had all antiquity been lost')

See note above to *To Mary, Lady Wroth* ('*How well, fair crown ...*').
8–9 *Ceres* Ceres (Demeter) was the daughter of Chronos and Rhea, and the elder sister of Zeus. She is the goddess of grain.
10 *Oenone* a nymph and wife of Paris.
 Flora Roman goddess of flowers.
 May Italian goddess, sometimes seen as an earth goddess.
11 *the Idalian queen* Venus.
16 *Pallas' pluméd casque* Pallas Athena (Minerva) is the goddess of wisdom, but usually represented in armour (*casque* = 'helmet') since in early Greek mythology she is best known as a warrior.
18 *Juno ... peacock* Juno (Hera) was the daughter of Chronos and Rhea, and wife of her brother Zeus. The peacock is her sacred bird.

To a Weak Gamester in Poetry

18–22 Jonson here uses several terms from the then popular card game of primero: *pluck* = 'draw a card'; *never art encountered* = 'you never have the right colour or suit'; *rest* = 'remaining stake'; *prime* = 'winning hand'.

To Mrs Philip Sidney

Title *Mrs* is here the formal 'mistress' and not referring to a married person. This lady (1594–1620) was the daughter of Robert Sidney, first Earl of Leicester; *Philip* was her baptismal name.

Epitaph on S.P., a Child of Q[ueen] El[izabeth's] Chapel

Title *S.P.* Salomon Pavy, one of the Children of Queen Elizabeth's Revels, acted in Jonson's *Cynthia's Revels* and died in 1602.

Epitaph on Elizabeth, L.H.

None of the surviving manuscripts gives any clue to the identity of this Elizabeth.

On the Famous Voyage

Title written *c.* 1610.

3 *the Latin muse* Virgil.

4 *Troy's just knight* Aeneas.

5 *Shelton . . . Heyden* Sir Ralph Shelton, who was knighted in 1607 and who had a contemporary reputation as a buffoon; Heyden has not been identified.

7–8 *Styx . . . Phlegeton* rivers in Hell.

8 *one* i.e., the Fleet Ditch.

20 *adventer* adventure.

21 *wights* men.

27–8 *gave . . . His three for one* paid a dividend of three to one in profits on investments for the voyage.

30 *shoon* shoes.

35 *him that backward . . . Berwick* unidentified.

36 *famous . . . Norwich* Will Kemp, the actor, danced from London to Norwich in 1599.

39 *his to Bristo'* Richard Ferris rowed in a wherry from Tower Wharf to Bristol in 1590.

40   *his to Antwerp*   who did this has not been identified.

50   *Alcides*   Hercules.

55   *Great club-fist*   Hercules.

62   *Ycleped*   called.

89   *How hight the place?*   'What is the place called?'

95   *ab excelsis*   from on high.

102   *cataplasms*   plasters, poultices.

115   *sough*   sigh.
      lurden   something heavy or worthless.

117   In the early seventeenth century the Butchers' Company used to send offal by boat for the King's bears.

120   *foist*   barge, with a pun on 'foist' ('foul smell').

128   *Democrite . . . Hill Nicholas*   Democritus (born *c.* 460 BC) was the founder of the theory of atoms; Nicholas Hill (?1570–1610) was a follower of Democritus.

133   *nare*   nostril.

155   *Tiberts*   Tibert is the name of the cat in the fable of Reynard the fox: here a generic name for cats.

156   *Banks*   exhibited his horse Morocco in the 1580s and 1590s. Banks was not dead in 1625 as Jonson implies.

190   *purblind fletcher*   a completely blind maker of arrows.

196   *his . . . A-JAX*   a reference to Sir John Harington (1561–1612), writer of epigrams, translator of Ariosto, author of a witty treatise on water-closets (= jakes): hence the pun on jakes and Ajax.

THE FOREST

This collection was first published in the 1616 folio *Works*. The title is an English version of the Latin 'silva', used for collections of occasional poems.

Why I Write Not of Love

Written *c.* 1611–12.

To Penshurst

Written before November 1612. At the time of this poem Penshurst (Kent) was the home of Robert, brother of Sir Philip Sidney. Robert Sidney was knighted in 1586, created Viscount Lisle in 1605 and Earl of Leicester in 1618.

2 *touch*   black marble.
14 *his great birth*   that of Sir Philip Sidney in 1554.
19 *Gamage*   Barbara Gamage married Lord Sidney in 1584.
36 *Officiously*   dutifully.
48 *clown*   peasant.
73 *livery*   here, provision.
79 *Penates*   Roman household gods.
91 *thy great lord*   Robert Sidney.

To Sir Robert Wroth

Written before 1615.
Title   Wroth (1576–1614) was knighted in 1601 and connected with the Sidney family by marriage. His country house was Durrants, in Enfield, and Wroth was a prominent Parliamentarian.
44 *mast*   acorn-eating.
48 *Comus*   pseudo-pagan god of revelry.
50 *Saturn's reign*   the age of gold.
61 *leese*   lose.
79 *blow up*   ruin.
95 *a strange shelf*   the idea seems to be that God does not want anyone to be ruined, or to die, away from home.

To the World
(A Farewell for a Gentlewoman, Virtuous and Noble)

Title   The gentlewoman of the title has not been identified and may well be fictitious.
24 *gyves*   fetters, chains.
31 *wull*   will.
36 *gins*   traps.
45 *soil*   i.e., place (?the Court).
56 *grutch*   complain.

Song. To Celia ('*Come my Celia, let us prove*')

This lyric appears also in *Volpone* (1606), III. 7. 166–83.

To the Same

22 *pined* pained.

To Sickness

3 *ynow* enough.
9 *stalls* alms-house lodgings.
10 *Spittles* here, leper hospitals.
  pest-house hospital for victims of the plague or smallpox.
31 *emp'rics* quacks, charlatans.
38 *stew* brothel.
41 *common game* promiscuously.

'And must I sing? What subject shall I choose?'

This, together with *Epode*, was printed in Robert Chester's *Love's Martyr* (1601).
4–5 The reference is to the twelve labours Eurystheus imposed on Hercules.
7 *cart* chariot.
17 *tribade trine* (a) the three Graces; (b) Lesbians.
19 *the old boy, your son* the idea that Cupid is both the youngest and the oldest god is a Platonic one.
22 *Hermes, the cheater* Hermes is, among other things, the god of rogues and thieves.
24 *Petasus* (Greek 'petasos') a broad-brimmed hat, one of Hermes' identifying features.
25 *ladies of the Thespian lake* the Muses. The Thespian lake is Aganippe, on the Helicon.

Epistle to Elizabeth, Countess of Rutland

Title Elizabeth, daughter of Sir Philip Sidney, married Roger Manners, fifth Earl of Rutland, and died in 1612. The poem is a New Year's gift for 1600.
9 *huishers* ushers.
29 *Turn . . . their quarter-face* turn almost completely away in aversion.
52 *Or, in an army's* Or, at the head of an army, encased in armour.
54 *Idomen* Idomeneus, Cretan captain at Troy.

58 *the Tyndarides* Castor and Pollux.

61 *Berenice* wife to Ptolemy III.

62 *Cassiopea* mother of Andromeda.

66 *Lucina ... Lucy the bright* Queen Elizabeth ... Lucy, Countess of Bedford.

92 *your brave friend* the Earl of Rutland.

Epistle. To Katherine, Lady Aubigny

Written 1611–12.

Title Katherine was daughter of Sir Gervase Clifton and married Esmé, Seigneur d'Aubigny, in 1609. She died in 1627.

33 *taken up o'* bought from.

39 *cozening farmer of the customs* a cheating tax-collector (who paid a set sum to his appointee for what he was able to collect and was allowed to keep the surplus).

72 *Maintain ... forth* having agents abroad able to provide the newest fashions.

102 *triple trine* nine months. A trine is a threefold unit.

Ode. To Sir William Sidney, on His Birthday

Written 1611–12.

Title William Sidney (son of Robert, nephew to Philip, grandchild of Sir Henry Sidney) was born in 1590, knighted in 1610 and died in 1612.

UNDERWOODS

The collection from which this selection comes was first printed as part of the two-volume folio put out by Kenelm Digby in 1640, after Jonson's death. There are signs of purposive grouping, but it is not clear how far the arrangement reflects Jonson's own wishes. His note 'To the Reader' indicates that he at least planned the collection, and Jonson says that he has given the title *Underwoods* for 'these lesser poems of later growth ... out of the analogy they hold to the *Forest* ...'

A Celebration of Charis in Ten Lyric Pieces

1 'HIS EXCUSE FOR LOVING'

Written in 1623. The other lyrics may well be earlier. Certainly the fourth, which appears in *The Devil is an Ass*, had been written by 1616.

4 'HER TRIUMPH'
28 *nard* spikenard, an aromatic ointment.

5 'HIS DISCOURSE WITH CUPID'
35 *proin* preen.
41 *girdle 'bout her waist* in Homer the goddess of love has a magic girdle of aphrodisiac power.

8 'URGING HER OF A PROMISE'
23 *purl* lace border.
25 *secretary Sis* confidential attendant.

9 'HER MAN DESCRIBED BY HER OWN DICTAMEN'
13 *more slack* duller.
40 *brake* framework.

My Picture Left in Scotland

Written in 1619.
7 *close* in music, the conclusion of a strain or movement.
8 *sentence* meaning, substance.

An Epistle to Sir Edward Sackville, now Earl of Dorset

Title Sackville (1591–1652) became fourth Earl of Dorset in 1624.
45 *air, or print* spoken or written thanks.
63 *was made* i.e., was knighted.
74 *at still* nevertheless.
101 *Rear-suppers* meals later than evening dinner.
156 *indice* indicator.

An Epistle to Master John Selden

Title Selden (1584–1654) was a jurist and friend to Jonson. This poem (1614) was prefixed to Selden's *Titles of Honour*.
21 *terms* limits.
58 *colours* rhetorical figures.
72 *chamber-fellow* Edward Hayward (1600–58).
80 *comings in* benefits, income.
81 *grain* character, quality.

An Epistle to a Friend, to Persuade Him to the Wars

Title   the friend is named as Colby in l. 176 but is otherwise unidentified. The wars of the title are presumably the European religious conflicts of the period.

37   *capital*   our most prominent concern.

56   *leese*   lose.

67   *pound a prick*   excite the male organ sexually.

69   *cast*   vomit.

70   *pickardil*   a large and fashionable collar.

71   *brise*   gadfly.

76   *saut*   salt, in the sense of salacious.

80   *Pitts, or Wright, or Modet*   clearly contemporary whores of some reputation.

86   This refers to a commercial activity in which the borrower was forced to take part or all of a loan in merchandise: he could try to resell it, but the given material was usually unsellable.

105   *Counters ... Fleet*   both prisons, the Counters being specifically for debtors.

107   *foot-cloth*   a horse's ornamented cloth.

174   *muster-master*   a person charged with taking account of troops.

Epistle to a Friend

Title   The friend has not been identified.

7   *protested be*   have liability alleged against me.

9   *band*   bond.

15   *Venter*   venture, speculate.

An Elegy ('By those bright eyes . . .')

3   *stand*   a platform or standing-point for shooting at game.

4   *double bow*   each of the mistress's eyebrows is seen as a Cupid's bow.

An Ode ('High-spirited friend . . .')

1   *friend*   the friend has not been identified.

2   *corsives*   used here with the sense of 'antiseptics'.

18   *husband*   husbandman, conserver.

An Elegy ('’Tis true, I’m broke . . .’)

27   *arraigned*   called to account.
      cast   discarded, condemned.
62   *starve*   kill (Old English ‘steorfan’).
99   *chore*   company (Latin ‘chorus’).

An Elegy ('Let me be what I am . . .’)

16   *purl*   ornamental loop of fabric.
29–31   This seems to refer to Jonson’s involvement with masques.
42   *preoccupy*   make use of before others.
43   *Put a coach-mare in tissue*   dress a coach-horse in fine thread.
50   *brave*   well-dressed.
71   *the Spittle sermon*   a sermon preached near the site of the old hospital of St Mary Spittle of Bishopsgate Without.
75   *l’envoy*   conclusion.
84   *close-stool*   a closed box with a chamber pot inside.
85   *scabbard*   dress.

An Execration upon Vulcan

The occasion of this poem was the burning of Jonson’s library in 1623.
8   *closed in horn*   cuckolded (by Mars); in a horn lantern.
29   *Amadis de Gaul*   romance by Montalvo (1510), translated by Munday (1618–19).
30   *Esplandians*   Esplandian was the son of Amadis and Oriana.
      Palmerins   *Palmerin d’Oliva*, a French version of a Spanish romance, was translated by Munday (1588, 1597). *Palmerin of England* (1596, 1602) was translated from French versions of Portuguese originals.
34   *logogriphs*   OED defines as ‘A kind of enigma, in which a certain word, and other words that can be formed out of all or any of its letters, are to be guessed from synonyms of them introduced into a set of verses’.
36   *eteostichs*   (chronograms) are sentences in which certain letters (usually capitalized) when run together give a date in Roman numerals.
      flammes   conceits.
39   *telestichs*   in these the final letters of the various words spell out a word or name.
66   *the Legend*   the *Legenda Aurea*, a thirteenth-century compilation of saints’ lives by Voragine.

69–70 *Turpins . . . Rolands . . . Oliveers* major figures in the French romance *The Song of Roland*.

69 *the Peers* the twelve Peers of Christendom.

71 *his cabal's loss* the Rosicrucians linked their doctrines with the mystical lore of the rabbis – the cabbala.

77 Nicholas Breton's *Pasquil* pamphlets were published 1600–1602, but 'Meddle with your match' has not been traced.

79 *Captain Pamphlet* refers, it seems, to a Captain Gainford, soldier and voluminous pamphleteer.

81 *weekly corrants* Nathaniel Butter's weekly newsletters, published from St Paul's churchyard.

82 *the prophet Ball* John Ball, tailor-turned-preacher.

89–90 *Venusine . . . Stagerite* i.e., a translation of Horace's *Ars Poetica* with material from Aristotle's *Poetics*.

91 *the Grammar* Jonson rewrote this and it was published in 1640.

96 *the Sicilian maid* a Latin romance of that name by Buchanan.

100 *Carew* Richard Carew (1555–1620) the antiquary.
      Cotton Sir Robert Cotton (1571–1631), antiquary and librarian.
      Selden John Selden (1584–1654), jurist.

101 *humanity* observations on the human condition.

103 *the Fathers* the early Church Fathers.
      wiser guides presumably pre-Reformation commentators.

118–19 The reference is to John Squire's *Triumph of Peace* for the 1620 Lord Mayor's Show.

123 *the Bankside* the Surrey shore of the Thames.

132 *the Globe* burnt down in 1613.

139 *The Brethren* publishers of reports and ballads dealing with the fire.

142 *the Winchestrian goose* venereal disease.

148 *the nun, Kate Arden* a famous whore (nun = whore is a famous double meaning in the sixteenth and seventeenth centuries).

149 *Kindled the fire* caught venereal disease.

153 *Fortune* the Fortune theatre was burnt down in 1621.

156 *Whitehall* the Whitehall banqueting house was burnt in 1618.

160 In Homer Hephaestus/Vulcan was on the Greek side, while Venus was a Trojan supporter.

168 'You have uttered (*vented*) your wish to destroy but have not really succeeded.'

169 *the Rolls* the office of the Rolls was burnt in 1621.

180 *dye-fats* dyers' vats.

187 *bellman's lantern* the public-crier was also a night-watchman.

193 *Paul's steeple* burnt in 1561.

194 *fireworks … Ephesus* the temple of Diana there was burnt down in 356 BC.

195 *Alexandria* the library there was burnt down in AD 640.

198 *glaives* lances or swords.

199 *Bilbo* Bilbao, famous Spanish sword-making city.

201 *the friar* Roger Bacon (*c.* 1210–92) was an early empiricist, often seen as a black magician in the Renaissance. Tradition links his name with the invention of gunpowder.

216 *Bess Braughton* a famous and expensive whore who died of venereal disease.

A Speech according to Horace

Title 'Speech' has the sense of Latin 'sermo', used by Horace to indicate a conversational poem.

5 *Gondomar* Spanish ambassador to England, here linked with Aesop and thus 'a teller of diplomatic fables'.

20 *Swinnerton* a captain in the Honourable Artillery Company.

21 The reference is to the training days of the soldiers of whom Jonson is writing. Pimlico was fortified as part of their manoeuvres.

28 *posture book* a book about military drill and bearing.

30 *Flushing, or the Brill* these towns were handed over to Elizabeth as guarantees of the repayment of English expenses incurred in Leicester's Netherlands expedition of 1586–7.

33–4 Sir Hugh Hamersley was colonel of the Company in 1619 and its president from 1619 to 1633. Edward Panton was captain in the Company from 1612 to 1618, but Hamersley did not follow him as colonel.

38 *Tilly* Johann Tzerelaes, Count of Tilly (1559–1632), an important general on the Catholic side in the Thirty Years War.

41 *Maurice* Maurice, Prince of Orange.

42 *Spinola* Ambrosio Spinola (1569–1630) attacked Bergen-op-Zoom in 1622 and besieged Breda (1624–5).

81 *Guy, or Bevis* Guy of Warwick and Bevis of Hampton; both heroes of medieval romances.

99 *tailors' blocks* tailors' dummies.

An Epistle answering to One that Asked to be Sealed of the Tribe of Ben

Title *Tribe of Ben* the Biblical phrase (*Revelation* vii, 8) is here applied to Jonson's followers or 'sons'. The recipient of this poem has not been traced.

32 *the Valtelline* a valley in the Grisons which formed a strategically important route for Spanish troops heading for Italy. The French captured it in 1624.

33 *States'* the Dutch.

33–6 The reference is to the dispensation to allow Charles to marry the Spanish Infanta.

44 *Brunsfield, and Mansfield* the former is unidentified, but the latter is Ernest, Count of Mansfield, who commanded the army of Frederick, Elector Palatine.

48 This refers to the futile arrangements for the reception of the Infanta.

64 *well-tagged* well fastened.

An Epigram on the Court Pucell

Title *Pucell* = maid, virgin, but by this time also slut or whore. The pucell here is Cecelia Bulstrode, who died in 1609.

7 *tribade* Lesbian.

8 *epicoene* having characteristics of both sexes.

40 *fits o'th'mother* hysterics; also punning on the idea of inviting lords and sermoneers to father a child on her.

42 *Dorrel's deed* John Dorrel (a preacher and exorcist) was gaoled in 1599 following a case involving William Sommers of Nottinghamshire.

To Master John Burges

Title Burges was one of the clerks of the Exchequer.

4 *Sir Robert Pie* he held the title of Treasurer's Remembrancer from 1618 and was knighted in 1621.

6 *debentur* a writing acknowledging a debt.

26 This means, I think, that if no help is forthcoming the poet will have to go on poor relief.

An Epigram. To William, Earl of Newcastle

Title William Cavendish (1592–1676), Earl of Newcastle (1628) wrote verse, was a famous horseman, a great landowner, and a

Royalist general in the Civil War. He wrote *The Truth of the Sorde* on fencing.

An Epigram. To K[ing] Charles for a Hundred Pounds He Sent Me in My Sickness. 1629.

Title The money seems to have been sent following the failure of *The New Inn*.

4 *King's evil* scrofula, which was supposed to be cured by a monarch's touch.

10 Everyone touched for the *King's evil* received an angel (ten shillings) so that Jonson's £100 = 200 angels.

14 Parliament was dissolved in 1629 because of deteriorating relationships with Charles I.

An Ode, or Song, by All the Muses

4–9 Referring, it would seem, to the Queen's unpopularity.

7 *2 Mel.* Melpomene.

13 *3 Thal.* Thalia.

17 *theorbo* a two-necked lute-type instrument.

19 *4 Eut.* Euterpe.

25 *5 Terp.* Terpsichore.

26 *Harry!* Henri IV of France.

27 *Lewis!* Louis XIII of France.

31 *6 Erat.* Erato.

36 *Ceston* Venus' girdle.

37 *7 Calli.* Calliope.

38 Competitors tilted at a metal ring suspended from a beam.

43 *8 Ura.* Urania.

46 *the play* Thomas Randolph's *Amyntas*.

49 *9 Poly.* Polyhymnia.

54 *a Caroline* a successor to Charles.

To the Immortal Memory and Friendship of that Noble Pair, Sir Lucius Cary and Sir H. Morison

Title Lucius Cary (?1610–43), second Viscount Falkland, was famous for his learning. Henry Morison was knighted in 1627 and died two years later.

THE TURN
Jonson uses the terms *Turn, Counter-Turn, Stand* to render the structural features of Pindar's Greek odes.
3-4 The Second Punic war began with Hannibal's capture of Saguntum in 219 BC.
89 *asterism* constellation.
93 *the Dioscuri* the twins Castor and Pollux.

To the Right Honourable, the Lord High Treasurer of England. An Epistle Mendicant. 1631

Title Richard, Lord Weston (1577-1635) became Treasurer in 1628 and Earl of Portland in 1632.
7 *false braies* artificial walls in front of the main walls.
8 *Reduicts* redoubts.
  half-moons 'demilunes' – crescent-shaped fortifications.
  horn-works outworks consisting of two half-bastions.

MISCELLANEOUS POEMS

To the Reader

From the Shakespeare first folio of 1618.
1 *This figure* the Droeshout portrait on the title-page of the folio.

To the Memory of My Beloved, the Author Mr William Shakespeare: And What He Hath Left Us

5 *suffrage* agreement.
7 *seeliest* blindest (basically a term from falconry).
29 *Lyly* the dramatist John Lyly (?1554-1606).
30 *sporting Kyd* the dramatist Thomas Kyd (1558-1595). *Sporting* is a pun on Kyd (kid meaning 'little goat').
35 *Pacuvius, Accius* the former (*c.* 220 to *c.* 130 BC) was a Roman tragic writer; the latter (170 to *c.* 86 BC) was also a writer of tragedies.
  him of Cordova dead Seneca the younger, born in Cordoba in Spain, whose tragedies had such influence on the Elizabethan theatre.
36-7 *buskin ... socks* the *buskin* is the English equivalent to the classical 'cothurnus' (the footwear for tragedies); while *socks* is an anglicized version of 'soccus' (the light slipper of the comic actor).
68 *true-filéd* truly polished.

The Vision of Ben Jonson, on the Muses of His Friend M. Drayton

Prefixed to Drayton's *The Battle of Agincourt* ... (1627), a volume which contained several of the poems Jonson mentions.

10 *conferring symbols* comparing tallies. The reference is to the Greek custom whereby parties to a contract broke a token in half, each keeping a piece.

20 *regions seven* Drayton's volume had seven headings on its title page.

25 *Legends three* *Piers Gaveston* (1593/4), *Matilda* (1594) and *Robert Duke of Normandy* (1596).

29 *Heroic Songs* *England's Heroicall Epistles* (1597).

32 *Naso* Ovid.

34 *the wise Athenian Owl* Drayton's *The Owl* (1604) is linked with Minerva (*the wise Athenian* = the wise owl of Athene/Minerva) because that bird was her emblem.

36 *volary* a large bird-cage.

50 *periegesis* literally *circumduction* (l. 51) = travels around.

61 *Thy catalogue of ships* in *The Battle of Agincourt*.

68 *Tyrtaeus* a Spartan poet of the seventh century BC.

86 *Lapland ... Cobalus* Lapland was famous for its witches; German 'kobold' = a mine-demon.

87 *Empusa, Lamia* Empusa is a demon in Aristophanes' *The Frogs*; Lamia is a child-eating ogre.

89 *thy ends* the elegies at the end of the 1627 volume.

Ode to Himself

This poem was provoked by the failure of Jonson's play *The New Inn* in 1629.

13 *fury* madness.

18 *draff* dregs.

23 *the shrieve's crust* the reference is to gaol food; *shrieve* means 'sheriff'.

27 *Broome's sweepings* Richard Brome (died ?1652) was a dramatist and follower of Jonson.

33 *orts* scraps.

42 *the Alcaic lute* Alcaeus was a lyric poet of the sixth or seventh century BC. He was born on Lesbos.

A Song of the Moon

This poem may perhaps have been part of the masque *The Gypsies Metamorphosed* at some stage in its composition.

1   *the wonders of the Peak*   St Anne's Well, Eldon Hole, Poole Hole.
15   *Morts*   women (a gypsy word).
     mirkins   malkins, slatterns.
27   *standard*   ensign.

A Panegyre, on the Happy Entrance of James, Our Sovereign, to His First High Session of Parliament in This Kingdom, the 19 of March, 1603

16   *damps*   poisonous vapours.
20   *Themis*   personification of justice.
24   *Dice*   Justice.
     Eunomia   Order.
27   *Irene*   peace.
40   *red*   perhaps Jonson means 'ashamed at their lack of articulation' (?).
47   *four . . . before*   James had made a progress through London on 15 March.
53   *this town*   Westminster (as distinct from London).
72   *tempered*   combined.
129   *eyne*   eyes.
130   *Iris*   daughter of Thaumas and Electra; goddess of the rainbow.
144–5   *greater bodies . . . lesser fires*   sun, moon . . . stars, planets.
145   *access*   approach, or – slightly metaphorically – rising.
153–4   *the artillery | Of heaven*   thunder.
motto   'Only the king and the poet are not of everyday birth' (Florus).

Over the Door at the Entrance into the Apollo

Title   The Apollo was the room in the Devil Tavern where Jonson drank with his friends.
3   *pottle*   a two-quart tankard.
4   *tripos*   a three-legged vessel.
8   A reference to Simon Wardlow, the tavern keeper (*skinker* = tapster).

An Expostulation with Inigo Jones

This is one of several poems about Jones. The two men worked together on a number of masques, but quarrelled about whose contribution should have priority on the title pages of the printed texts of *Love's Triumph* and *Chlorida*.

2 *pipkins* commodities, goods.

4 *Euclid* the Greek geometrician (*fl. c.* 300 BC).

5 *Archimede* (*c.* 287–212 BC) mathematician, astronomer, inventor.

   Architas (*fl. c.* 400 BC) philosopher and geometrician, said to have invented the screw and pulley.

7 *Ctesibius* Alexandrian engineer of about 250 BC.

8 *Vitruvius* first century BC; author of *De Architectura*.

13 *antics* grotesque costumes.

16 *tire-man, mountebank* dresser, charlatan.

   Justice Jones Jones was a Westminster J.P. from 1630.

20 *asinigo* little ass (with play on Inigo).

22 *Langley* Francis Langley built the Swan Theatre.

26 *sheath* scabbard.

27 *wooden dagger* a property of the Vice in morality plays.

60 *Skeuopoios* preparer of stage properties.

64–5 *dominus-do-| All* 'magister factotum'.

66 *whistle* parasite.

72 *lantern-lerry* a device for producing artificial light.

   fuliginous sooty, smoky.

79 *firk* jerk, jump.

   Adam Overdo the incompetent justice in *Bartholomew Fair*.

94 *cinnopar* crimson.

99 *the Worthies* the nine Worthies of Christendom.

101 *the Feasting Room* at Whitehall, burnt down in 1619.

104 *remonstrance* formal rebuke.

SONGS FROM JONSON'S PLAYS

'Slow, slow, fresh fount, keep time with my salt tears'

From *Cynthia's Revels* (1600–1601). Sung by Echo in I.2 and set to music by Youll in 1608.

'Queen and huntress, chaste, and fair'

From *Cynthia's Revels*; sung by Hesperus to Diana in V.6.

'Fools, they are the only nation'

From *Volpone* (1606); sung by Nano and Castrone in I.2.

'Still to be neat, still to be dressed'

From *Epicoene* (1609); sung by a boy in I.1 and set to music by William Lawes for a revival in 1665.
11 *adulteries* adulterations.

'My masters and friends, and good people draw near'

From *Bartholomew Fair* (1614); sung by Nightingale in III.5 to the tune of 'Peggington's Pound', the ballad being interspersed with prose comment.
18 *Westminster Hall* where courts of Common Law and Chancery sat.
40 One John Selman was executed in 1612 for doing this.

'It was a beauty that I saw'

Sung by Lovel in IV.4 of *The New Inn*.

SONGS FROM JONSON'S MASQUES AND ENTERTAINMENTS

Epithalamion

From *The Haddington Masque* 'at court, on the Shrove Tuesday at night, 1608'. The marriage was between John Ramsey, Viscount Haddington (*c.* 1580–1626) and Elizabeth Radcliffe, daughter of the Earl of Sussex. She died in 1616. Ferrabosco set ll. 45–54.

Charm

From *The Masque of Queens*. 'At Whitehall, February 2, 1609'. This is the third of the masque's nine charms.
2 *cat-a-mountain* wildcat.
14 *little Martin* the *little Martin* of the witches who calls them to conventicles.

'Buzz, quoth the blue-fly'

From *Oberon the Fairy Prince. A Masque of Prince Henry's* (1611). A 'catch' sung by satyrs and set by Edmund Nelham in 1667.
7–8   *He . . . he*   referring to two 'sylvan' in the masque.

'Now, my cunning lady moon'

From *Oberon*.
3   *the boy*   Endymion, beloved of Selene (the moon in Greek mythology).

'What just excuse had agèd Time'

From *Love Freed from Ignorance and Folly*.

'O how came Love, that is himself a fire'

From *Love Restored* (1612).

'Soft, subtle fire, thou soul of art'

From *Mercury Vindicated* (1616): 'A cyclop, tending the fire, to the cornets began to sing'.

'Hum drum, sauce for a cony'

From *Christmas, His Masque* (1616): sung by the figure of Christmas.
1   *cony*   rabbit, but also dupe and whore.
3   *stake*   the pole for dancing around.
6   *roll*   bustle.
15   *Tom of Bosom's Inn*   a London tavern where carriers stayed.
22   *kill-pot*   a solid drinker.
29   *trace*   line.
36   *Pur Alley*   not a street, but a pun on 'purale', meaning a 'survey'.

'Break, Fant'sy, from thy cave of cloud'

From *The Vision of Delight*, 'presented at court in Christmas, 1617'.

Hymn

From *Pleasure Reconciled to Virtue*, 'presented at court before King James, 1618'. This 'Hymn' opens the masque.

5   *hopper*   the funnel in a mill into which the grain is poured.
6   *hutch*   bin.
    boulter   sifter.
7   *bavin*   bundle of stove or oven wood.
    mawkin   baker's mop.
    peel   baker's shovel.
11   *Hippocras bag*   a cloth-filter used in straining wine.

'From the famous Peak of Derby'

From *The Gypsies Metamorphosed* (1621); sung by the Jackman. Nicholas Lanier composed the music for this masque and the song was also set by Robert Johnson.

2   *the Devil's Arse*   a cavern in Castleton, Derbyshire.
4   *Egyptians*   gypsies.
16   i.e., 'will not make ladies faint'.
23   *Burleigh*   where the first performance was held.

'The fairy beam upon you'

From *The Gypsies Metamorphosed* (1621).
5   *fire-drake*   probably 'meteor'.

'Cocklorrel woulds needs have the devil his guest'

From *The Gypsies Metamorphosed*; sung by the Jackman.
1   *Cocklorrel*   a term for an outstanding rogue.
6   *crudities*   undigested matter.
11   *Promoter*   informer.
15   *bawd*   the culinary meaning here is 'hare'.
18   *tirewomen*   dressmakers.
20   *sallet*   salad.
36   *hinch-boys*   pages.
43   *pettitoes*   basically pig's trotters.
51   *sippits*   croutons.
63   *flirted*   flicked.

Ballad

From *The Masque of Augurs*, 'presented on Twelfth Night, 1622'.

9 *St Katherine* an area of London around the Tower where the performers of the first anti-masque are said to come from. It was known for its breweries.

22 *Vintry Cranes* a public house in a part of London known as the Vintry.

24 *the Devil* a tavern near Temple Bar.

34–5 A Catherine Wheel decorated the gate mentioned in l. 34.

36 This odd piece of local history/legend crops up in several places, but has not been pinned down to any known incident.

47 *single coin* small change.

48 *budget* leather bag.

54 *jordan* chamber pot.

INDEX OF FIRST LINES

INDEX OF TITLES

FOR THE BEST IN PAPERBACKS, LOOK FOR THE 🐧

In every corner of the world, on every subject under the sun, Penguin represents quality and variety – the very best in publishing today.

For complete information about books available from Penguin – including Puffins, Penguin Classics and Arkana – and how to order them, write to us at the appropriate address below. Please note that for copyright reasons the selection of books varies from country to country.

In the United Kingdom: Please write to *Dept E.P., Penguin Books Ltd, Harmondsworth, Middlesex, UB7 0DA.*

If you have any difficulty in obtaining a title, please send your order with the correct money, plus ten per cent for postage and packaging, to *PO Box No 11, West Drayton, Middlesex*

In the United States: Please write to *Dept BA, Penguin, 299 Murray Hill Parkway, East Rutherford, New Jersey 07073*

In Canada: Please write to *Penguin Books Canada Ltd, 2801 John Street, Markham, Ontario L3R 1B4*

In Australia: Please write to the *Marketing Department, Penguin Books Australia Ltd, P.O. Box 257, Ringwood, Victoria 3134*

In New Zealand: Please write to the *Marketing Department, Penguin Books (NZ) Ltd, Private Bag, Takapuna, Auckland 9*

In India: Please write to *Penguin Overseas Ltd, 706 Eros Apartments, 56 Nehru Place, New Delhi, 110019*

In the Netherlands: Please write to *Penguin Books Netherlands B.V., Postbus 3507, 1001 AH, Amsterdam*

In West Germany: Please write to *Penguin Books Ltd, Friedrichstrasse 10–12, D–6000 Frankfurt/Main 1*

In Spain: Please write to *Alhambra Longman S.A., Fernandez de la Hoz 9, E–28010 Madrid*

In Italy: Please write to *Penguin Italia s.r.l., Via Como 4, I-20096 Pioltello (Milano)*

In France: Please write to *Penguin Books Ltd, 39 Rue de Montmorency, F-75003 Paris*

In Japan: Please write to *Longman Penguin Japan Co Ltd, Yamaguchi Building, 2–12–9 Kanda Jimbocho, Chiyoda-Ku, Tokyo 101*

FOR THE BEST IN PAPERBACKS, LOOK FOR THE 🐧

PENGUIN CLASSICS

ANTHOLOGIES AND ANONYMOUS WORKS

The Age of Bede
Alfred the Great
Beowulf
A Celtic Miscellany
The Cloud of Unknowing and Other Works
The Death of King Arthur
The Earliest English Poems
Early Irish Myths and Sagas
Egil's Saga
The Letters of Abelard and Heloise
Medieval English Verse
Njal's Saga
Seven Viking Romances
Sir Gawain and the Green Knight
The Song of Roland

FOR THE BEST IN PAPERBACKS, LOOK FOR THE 🐧

PENGUIN CLASSICS

Saint Anselm	**The Prayers and Meditations**
Saint Augustine	**The Confessions**
Bede	**Ecclesiastical History of the English People**
Chaucer	**The Canterbury Tales**
	Love Visions
	Troilus and Criseyde
Marie de France	**The Lais of Marie de France**
Jean Froissart	**The Chronicles**
Geoffrey of Monmouth	**The History of the Kings of Britain**
Gerald of Wales	**History and Topography of Ireland**
	The Journey through Wales and The Description of Wales
Gregory of Tours	**The History of the Franks**
Henryson	**The Testament of Cresseid and Other Poems**
Walter Hilton	**The Ladder of Perfection**
Julian of Norwich	**Revelations of Divine Love**
Thomas à Kempis	**The Imitation of Christ**
William Langland	**Piers the Ploughman**
Sir John Mandeville	**The Travels of Sir John Mandeville**
Marguerite de Navarre	**The Heptameron**
Christine de Pisan	**The Treasure of the City of Ladies**
Marco Polo	**The Travels**
Richard Rolle	**The Fire of Love**
François Villon	**Selected Poems**

FOR THE BEST IN PAPERBACKS, LOOK FOR THE 🐧

PENGUIN CLASSICS

End Pages – gal. 26

FOR THE BEST IN PAPERBACKS, LOOK FOR THE

PENGUIN CLASSICS

Matthew Arnold	Selected Prose
Jane Austen	Emma
	Lady Susan, The Watsons, Sanditon
	Mansfield Park
	Northanger Abbey
	Persuasion
	Pride and Prejudice
	Sense and Sensibility
Anne Brontë	Agnes Grey
	The Tenant of Wildfell Hall
Charlotte Brontë	Jane Eyre
	Shirley
	Villette
Emily Brontë	Wuthering Heights
Samuel Butler	Erewhon
	The Way of All Flesh
Thomas Carlyle	Selected Writings
Wilkie Collins	The Moonstone
	The Woman in White
Charles Darwin	The Origin of Species
	The Voyage of the Beagle
Benjamin Disraeli	Sybil
George Eliot	Adam Bede
	Daniel Deronda
	Felix Holt
	Middlemarch
	The Mill on the Floss
	Romola
	Scenes of Clerical Life
	Silas Marner
Elizabeth Gaskell	Cranford and Cousin Phillis
	The Life of Charlotte Brontë
	Mary Barton
	North and South
	Wives and Daughters

FOR THE BEST IN PAPERBACKS, LOOK FOR THE 🐧

PENGUIN CLASSICS

William Hazlitt	**Selected Writings**
Thomas Hobbes	**Leviathan**

Samuel Johnson/
  James Boswell
	**A Journey to the Western Islands of
	  Scotland and The Journal of a Tour to the
	  Hebrides**

Charles Lamb	**Selected Prose**
Samuel Richardson	**Clarissa** **Pamela**
Richard Brinsley Sheridan	**The School for Scandal and Other Plays**
Christopher Smart	**Selected Poems**
Adam Smith	**The Wealth of Nations**
Tobias Smollett	**The Expedition of Humphry Clinker** **The Life and Adventures of Sir Launcelot Greaves**

Laurence Sterne	**The Life and Opinions of Tristram Shandy,
	  Gentleman**
	**A Sentimental Journey Through France and
	  Italy**

Jonathan Swift	**Gulliver's Travels**
Sir John Vanbrugh	**Four Comedies**

FOR THE BEST IN PAPERBACKS, LOOK FOR THE 🐧

PENGUIN CLASSICS

PLAYS IN PENGUIN

Edward Albee	**Who's Afraid of Virginia Woolf?**
Alan Ayckbourn	**The Norman Conquests**
Bertolt Brecht	**Parables for the Theatre (The Good Woman of Setzuan/The Caucasian Chalk Circle)**
Anton Chekhov	**Plays (The Cherry Orchard/Three Sisters/Ivanov/The Seagull/Uncle Vania)**
Henrik Ibsen	**Hedda Gabler/The Pillars of the Community/The Wild Duck**
Eugène Ionesco	**Rhinoceros/The Chairs/The Lesson**
Ben Jonson	**Three Comedies (Volpone/The Alchemist/Bartholomew Fair)**
D. H. Lawrence	**Three Plays (The Collier's Friday Night/The Daughter-in-Law/The Widowing of Mrs Holroyd)**
Arthur Miller	**Death of a Salesman**
John Mortimer	**A Voyage Round My Father/What Shall We Tell Caroline?/The Dock Brief**
J. B. Priestley	**Time and the Conways/I Have Been Here Before/An Inspector Calls/The Linden Tree**
Peter Shaffer	**Lettice and Lovage/Yonadab**
Bernard Shaw	**Plays Pleasant (Arms and the Man/Candida/The Man of Destiny/You Never Can Tell)**
Sophocles	**Three Theban Plays (Oedipus the King/Antigone/Oedipus at Colonus)**
Arnold Wesker	**Plays, Volume 1: The Wesker Trilogy (Chicken Soup with Barley/Roots/I'm Talking about Jerusalem)**
Oscar Wilde	**The Importance of Being Earnest and Other Plays (Lady Windermere's Fan/A Woman of No Importance/An Ideal Husband/Salome)**
Thornton Wilder	**Our Town/The Skin of Our Teeth/The Matchmaker**
Tennessee Williams	**Cat on a Hot Tin Roof/The Milk Train Doesn't Stop Here Anymore/The Night of the Iguana**

FOR THE BEST IN PAPERBACKS, LOOK FOR THE 🐧

PENGUIN BOOKS OF POETRY

American Verse
British Poetry Since 1945
Caribbean Verse in English
A Choice of Comic and Curious Verse
Contemporary American Poetry
Contemporary British Poetry
English Christian Verse
English Poetry 1918–60
English Romantic Verse
English Verse
First World War Poetry
Greek Verse
Irish Verse
Light Verse
Love Poetry
The Metaphysical Poets
Modern African Poetry
New Poetry
Poetry of the Thirties
Post-War Russian Poetry
Scottish Verse
Southern African Verse
Spanish Civil War Verse
Spanish Verse
Women Poets